THE POWER OF SPEECH

OF SPEECH

by Marie Stuttard

BARRON'S

First U.S. edition published in 1997 by Barron's Educational Series, Inc.

First published in 1995 by
David Bateman Limited
Tarndale Grove
Albany Business Park
Bush Road, Albany
AUCKLAND 1330
NEW ZEALAND

All inquiries should be addressed to:
Barron's Educational Series, Inc.
250 Wireless Boulevard
Hauppauge, New York 11788

Library of Congress Catalog Card No. 96-31877

International Standard Book No. 0-8120-9795-5

Library of Congress Cataloging-in-Publication Data
Stuttard, Marie.
    The power of speech / by Marie Stuttard.—1st U.S. ed.
        p.   cm.
    ISBN 0-8120-9795-5
    1. Speech.   2. Voice culture.   3. Elocution.   4. Oral
communication.   5. Public speaking.   I. Title.
PN4162.S727   1996
808.5—dc20   96-31877
                                                         CIP

Cover and book design by Marquerite van Bergen, Charisma Digital

Printed in Hong Kong
987654321

To Claire and Louise,
my darling granddaughters

CONTENTS

PREFACE

The Power of Speech is the result of a lifetime's experience as a teacher, lecturer, performer, and author.

Language is my passion!

Now I would like to pass on to you not only my passion for language—and speech in particular—but the professional tricks of the trade that may help you to become a speaker extraordinaire.

When I look back, I realize that when I gained my teacher's diploma from the Guildhall School of Speech and Drama, London, I was actually very young and inexperienced. It's taken many years to build the knowledge that I am able to offer now.

That experience comes from many quarters. It started, in Northern Ireland, when, at seven, I began lessons with a superb teacher, Hilda Taggart, herself an examiner at the Guildhall. Although I come from a family of orators, she instilled in me a great love of language that has remained with me all these years.

Through her I began broadcasting as a child and later took part in almost every aspect of radio, including drama, interviews, documentaries, poetry reading, and came to have a real affection for the medium. I learned the hard way, as most of the broadcasts were live rather than recorded.

When Northern Ireland B.B.C. television started, because of my experience, I was one of the first to be chosen and I enjoyed the excitement and stimulation of it all. I was involved too in the early days of television in New Zealand—the panel games, "advice" shows, and special programs such as a 13-part series, *Fashion is Fun*—based on my first book, as guest and host.

And, of course, speaking in public—presenting shows, lecturing, giving talks and so on—has always been second nature to me.

Woven into what I call my "speech days" were the "written" ones! I have been a journalist on a daily newspaper and on a weekly magazine, as well as a *Vogue* fashion editor. To date, I have had nine books published—mainly for children—so experience with the written word has been invaluable to my overall view of language.

A long time ago I began lecturing to the corporate world and this changed the way I thought about communication. Business people want to be improved yesterday—not tomorrow or next year. I held master classes that crammed people with information in the shortest possible time using video.

This is how I've tried to set out the information in *The Power of Speech*. I felt it had to be easy to read and quick to learn from, so that you don't have to plow through many pages before you get to a point.

There are no chapters. You can open it anywhere. Every two pages are complete in themselves. And it's meant to tell you not so much *what* to say as *how* to say it.

The book is designed to make you aware of the subtleties of speech, the intricacies of language, and the amazing qualities of the voice. But most of all it's to show that simple, flowing, eloquent language can lift you out of the rut of mediocrity and put you into the realm of the professional.

I hope you will get as much fun out of *The Power of Speech* as I've had writing it. I hope, too, that you'll gain from it and be able to put into practice some of its theories in your own unique way.

Marie Stuttard

NO MATTER HOW

Intelligent Knowledgeable Organized

Good-looking or Rich

we are,

the **CRUNCH** comes

when we have to

SPEAK!

CONTROLLING THE "CRUNCH"

We're all faced with the "crunch" at one time or another. Everybody knows people who really are intelligent, knowledgeable, educated, good-looking, or rich, yet when they speak, they let themselves down—sometimes badly. So, qualifications, money, or power alone won't necessarily turn you into an effective speaker. I'm using the word *speaker* in the widest sense, not just as in *public speaker,* but as a means of communicating every day of your life.

SKILLS IN A BOX

I don't believe in having speaking skills that you keep in a box and bring out only when the occasion demands. I was once a guest of a club that encourages public speaking. One of its members had just won a national title, and during the evening he repeated his winning speech for us. It was extremely good; carefully written and spoken with considerable ability. I was impressed and afterwards went to congratulate him. What happened? He muttered a few words and fled! He couldn't speak to me on a one-to-one basis. He was not a communicator. He had written, rehearsed, and presented his speech as an actor would. I was hoping he'd reply as he had spoken on stage—with personality—and was disappointed when he could not.

THE BIG BREEZE

On the other hand, I know many who, in private, are delightful speakers, with warm, witty, and interesting voices full of tonal variety. But put them on a platform and they freeze. I try to marry the two skills, so that in private or in public, people can speak naturally with vitality and eloquence.

As this is a do-it-yourself book, I would like you to become aware of *your* strengths and weaknesses by answering the following questions. Make a note of your answers so that you can refer to them later.

ASK YOURSELF

How do I rate as a speaker?

How CONFIDENT am I?

Am I fluent? EXPRESSIVE? persuasive?

Do I make an IMPACT on others?

Can I hold their attention?

Do I look NERVOUS?

Is my speech SLOPPY?

What makes me TONGUE-TIED?

Why am I often asked to repeat myself?

Do I BREATHE properly?

Do I mutter behind clenched teeth?

Why does my MIND go BLANK sometimes?

Do I jump from one subject to another?

Can people follow my REASONING?

Have I ever listened, really listened,
to the SOUND of my VOICE?

SELF-APPRAISAL

If you've answered all the questions faithfully (it's amazing how we can delude ourselves about our ability) you'll now have a better understanding of the quality of your speech and ability to communicate.

If some of your answers were negative, don't worry. Anyone at any age can improve. I've seen it happen over and over again. I believe most people need only a little help.

AVID LEARNERS

I was trained in the slow-but-sure method over years and years, but because I deal mainly with those in a hurry, I've devised a method that literally crams you with information and professional tricks of the trade in the shortest possible time.

I find that people who need to improve quickly are usually avid learners. If they have a good ear, they can pick up the sounds and rhythms of speech rapidly, and it always gives me great satisfaction to see immediate improvement and the confidence they gain.

DON'T STOP

If you feel you are already quite good, don't stop learning, for there is a wide gap between quite good and very good. The "quite" is amateurish, the "very" more professional. Say you have to give a speech or go to an interview. With no training at all, you can turn in a creditable performance, provided you're feeling well and your adrenalin is flowing. But if you're off color—have a headache perhaps, or you just feel nervous—you can do poorly. Next time you'll wonder if it'll be a repeat performance.

With the minimum of training, the cutoff point is "good." You can't be bad, for no matter how nervous or tense you are, your technique will carry you through. But if you're feeling well and your adrenalin is flowing you can be brilliant!

POINT TO PONDER

how can we

overcome

our

NERVES?

POSITIVE OR NEGATIVE

Negative nerves can almost destroy us, at least when speaking in public or even going to an interview. The anxiety, the palpitations, the sweaty hands—these are dead giveaways. Fear is a strange phenomenon. It breeds rapidly, has no social boundaries, can affect all age groups, and, if left alone to multiply, can have a damaging effect on the personality.

FREE OF FEAR

If we're determined to stay fear-bound, that's probably how we'll remain. But if there's that urge to spank it, chop its head off, kill it off forever, then we have to rely on *mental discipline.*

To do that we need to build a strong foundation: listen to speech, understand speech, analyze speech, practice speech, have faith in our speech. There's nothing like a little faith to combat fear.

When we're about to make a speech, we have to do our homework, know what we want to say, and plan it thoroughly. If we're going to an important interview, the buildup is much the same. A disorganized approach leaves us vulnerable. We need to know that up to the time we step onto the platform or into the office, we've got everything under control. That promotes confidence. We know we can't be bad.

We must have a positive approach—appear positive and feel positive.

IT'S ALL GO!

On that day, we have to make sure we look good—well dressed and groomed—so that we can forget about our appearance.

An irritating habit of nervous speakers is licking the lips because they get dry. To combat this, even men should put a light film of petroleum jelly on their lips. This takes away the urge to lick. Try it out beforehand.

I suggest putting two teaspoonfuls of sugar in a cup of tea and drinking it before you leave home. This gives instant energy and is great for calming the nerves.

When you arrive, it's head up, a big smile, and you're on your way!

IF WE SPEAK WELL
WE'RE LUCKY

The way we speak, the way we communicate,

can affect our whole career

If you're not happy with your voice

DON'T WORRY

It's surprising how quickly you can improve

if you really want to

By acquiring the ear for sound and absorbing the

professional tricks of the trade

you can do it in a

SURPRISINGLY

SHORT TIME

TRICKS OF THE TRADE

We talk glibly of such tricks, often not knowing exactly what they are. In this case, there would be too many to list because they pervade every aspect of our speech.

Nevertheless, they are there, all the time, in every sentence we utter, on every occasion. Even people who have no awareness of these so-called tricks often judge others as professionals because they instinctively sense what good speakers are without knowing why.

TELEPHONE TALK

Let's take a few examples.

A stranger telephones you. By the way he speaks, you get a quick impression of the kind of person you're talking to. If the caller sounds nervous, stumbles over words, or muddles up information, you're not too impressed, perhaps a little cautious. If the person has a harsh voice, is demanding or rather aggressive, you're on your guard.

But if the caller speaks well, confidently and with vitality, at least you're prepared to listen. I've even chatted with wrong number callers because of the delightful way they speak.

This doesn't necessarily mean they are what they sound like, of course. Con artists use every trick in the book to get what they want.

ONE WORD

It's hard to realize that we can be judged on just a few words. I'll take it even further and say that occasionally we only have to say *one* word and somebody is judging us.

How often have you judged someone on one word? The quality of her voice, the authority in it, the way it sounds, the tension, the warmth, perhaps the coldness, the sincerity. I know I frequently get instant impressions from one to a few words. As to the actual tricks themselves—*well, read this book!*

Think of yourself as a
SALESPERSON

We're constantly selling ourselves

WE SELL OUR

Personalities
Knowledge
Ideas
Desires
Plans
Products

WE SELL THEM TO OUR

Families
Friends
Neighbors
Acquaintances
Business Associates
and to the World in General

THE SALES PRESENTATION

When I tell people to think of themselves as salespeople, they do a double take. To them, salespeople are pushy and they don't want to be like that. But they've missed the point. We do sell ourselves, in a noncommercial way, every day, even to our nearest and dearest.

WHAT DO YOU DO?

If you want to convince your spouse that you need a new car, what do you do? You try to make your partner see that need through your eyes.

If you want your children to follow a particular schedule, what do you do? You use all your guile to present your proposition in such a way that your children will see it as exciting and interesting.

If you want to cut down a tree that lies on the property line between your house and your neighbor's, what do you do? You present your case in such a way that your neighbor sees the sense of it.

If you want people to sign a petition, join a club, or enter a competition, what do you do? You sell the idea to them, making it seem attractive and inviting.

In business, schemes, proposals, methods, ad infinitum, are being sold all the time.

If everyone was exceptionally good at selling, the world would be a much more stimulating place. Unfortunately, many are not and often they are those who really should be, including parents and educators.

INSPIRATION

"Bor-ing!" sigh the children after a class or a lecture from their parents. This is often because information is put to them in a dull, dreary way.

It's the same throughout life. We all need to be inspired. We work better when we are. In fact, an outstanding communicator can take any subject and make it interesting. While we can't all be outstanding, we can at least take our best shot at it.

Why are some people

more

PERSUASIVE

than others?

TRANSFERRING CONFIDENCE

We talk about the "art of persuasion"—and it is an art, a creative skill that uses language rather than a paintbrush or a pen.

How many times have we been intrigued by persuasive speakers? We're so overwhelmed by their fluency, the way they create their "word pictures," that we see what they see and want what they want us to want.

That's the strength of the art of persuasion. It's a highly desirable accomplishment. But how can we achieve success? Again, practice helps.

SELL

Start small. Take a book or a pen, any ordinary item, and try to "sell" it to someone, or even to yourself.

KNOW YOUR SUBJECT. Have all its good points ready to explain. Think out the best way to introduce them, emphasize them, use them.

Dig deeper by finding out the story behind the book, who wrote it and why, when it was published, what kind of reception it got, why it's still popular. Research the history of the pen. Find out how and when developments took place. Discover when the fountain pen was introduced, and the ballpoint, plus anything else you can think of. Always remember, if you want to be persuasive you must do your homework.

KNOW YOUR OBJECTIVE. If you're going to sell the item you must make the people you're selling to see that book, or pen, or whatever through your eyes. Don't be coy or too modest, those qualities irritate people. Sound realistic and enthusiastic. Present it in such a way that they feel they must have it immediately.

THE JACKPOT

When you can do that, go on to bigger topics. Sell someone the idea of getting a dog, trying a new diet, going on an overseas tour. Discover how you can transfer your confidence in anything to anyone. You've hit the jackpot when, through your art of persuasion, you can change people's opinion, sometimes even their lives.

Our ability to **communicate**

is often marred by some very

common faults

For instance

- A lazy speaker who mumbles often can't be heard

- A flat, monotonous, dreary voice makes us tune out—we can't help it

- A harsh voice is irritating

- Poor quality breathing results in poor quality speech

- A flabby tongue can't produce crisp speech

- A lot of "ums" and "ers" make speakers seem nervous and unsure of their facts

but

If you want to **improve** there's an easy way to do it
Learn the **basics of good speech** and apply them
EVERY DAY
You'll be amazed at your progress

FINDING FAULT

Finding fault with ourselves can be depressing, but it is part of our progress to good speech. If I had to choose the fault I find most irritating, I'd pick a *dull* voice. So much goes down the drain, so much excitement gets flattened, so much personality disappears when monotony creeps in. It's one of the great setbacks to a career, not to mention a social life. It's even important within the family.

HOW DO WE SOUND?

The funny thing is, while many people can recognize monotony in others, they don't always realize that their own voices are flat and uninteresting. This is because we've lived with our voices for so long, we seldom know what they sound like to others.

Of course, to be understood, first of all we have to be heard. Mumblers are frustrating to listen to. They don't open their mouths, their lips hardly move, their tongues are lazy, and their jaws seem to be locked into position.

Later in this book you'll find exercises to help all these conditions. There are exercises for breathing too—a vital ingredient in speech because poor breathing affects not only the quality of our voice but how we use it.

UMS AND ERS

The "ums and ers" syndrome is universal, yet there is a simple way to correct it. First of all, I want you to become *aware* of how good speech is produced, so that you can judge how *your* speech measures up. Brush up your ability to analyze; discover different ways and means of producing not only good speech, but the language itself in its most interesting form.

Then fine tune the areas where your speech needs attention. If these include the "ums and ers" do something about it without delay.

Start with a simple exercise. But before you begin, here's a tip: When doing any of the exercises in this book, remember that you'll improve quickly if you do them in small doses frequently rather than in large doses now and again.

POINT TO PONDER

how do we
get
rid of
"UMS" & "ERS"?

OUT THEY GO!

If there's any one thing that spoils a person's general speech, and speech making in particular, it's the "um," "er," "ah," "eh," "and a," "sort of," "kind of," "you know" syndrome.

Too many people shove these meaningless, silly little words into gaps when they run out of something to say, when they're nervous and can't think of what to say, and because they've done it for so long they don't know how to get rid of them.

So, if you "um" or "er" it's back to the drawing board.

A CURE

There's only one way I know of that helps you throw them away, shoot them down, drown them. *Every time you say them, or start to say them, stop! Say nothing.*

Always remember that a *pause* is far more effective.

Here again, we're back to mental discipline.

This is where the art of listening pays off. By now, I hope you've learned to listen and analyze your speech and speech patterns. If so, you'll be aware of how many times you resort to trivial insertions like these.

NOT NEEDED

They do absolutely nothing for your speech. They detract from its effectiveness. You've got to get rid of them *pronto!* Remember, only YOU can do it. No one else can do it for you.

People sometimes try to tell me that it's a way of speech and not necessarily a fault. Nonsense! They're covering up. Listen to top quality speakers of English from any country. Do they include an array of "um," "er," "ah," "eh," "and a," "sort of," "kind of," "you know" in their speech? Of course not. They wouldn't degrade their language.

While saying that, let me hasten to add that we all do the occasional one! But that's all it is, an occasional one.

Overall, speech doesn't need them.

Practice the way you say your

NAME

Because you're so familiar with your name,

it's easy to forget that

OTHER PEOPLE are NOT

Many people say their names

INDISTINCTLY

and

TOO QUICKLY

You need to *slow down* and

enunciate very clearly

YOUR NAME IS YOU

If this easy exercise was taught in schools we might be saved from continually having to ask adults to repeat their names.

Your name is precious to you. It's your identification, your passport, your individuality. It should always be spoken slowly enough and clearly enough so that others can actually *hear* it.

If I said, "I'mMarieStuttardofABCCompany," you'd say, "Who?" So I'd have to slow down and start again. Practice saying your name until you're sure it will be easy for people to understand, even if they are hearing it for the first time.

THE NEAT TRICK

Once you're satisfied, use the same technique *every time* you say your name, other people's names, company names, trade names, or any word your listeners might have difficulty picking up. It's a little trick, but it's sure to be appreciated.

Although the way you say your name is always important, obviously greater care has to be taken when using the *telephone*. The person on the other end of the line can't see you or watch your facial expression or body language. They have only your *voice* to make sense of what you say.

ON THE TELEPHONE

Sometimes I'm asked how operators should answer the telephone. Should they say, "ABC Company," "ABC Company, good morning," or "Good morning, ABC Company"? I prefer the latter. The "good morning" gives the caller a chance to tune into the operator's voice, then the company name comes across more easily.

We've all suffered at parties when the host or hostess has rattled off the names of the other guests incomprehensively. It leaves you quite bewildered. Inviting each guest to say his or her own name might help solve that problem, especially if each one speaks clearly.

There's something else that's important, too...

THE GREETING

THE FIRST VERBAL SIGNAL WE SEND OUT

A grumpy person might say, "GOOD MORNING"
The voice drops and sounds depressing

An uptight person might say, "GOOD MORNING"
Clipped and very precise

Most people say, "GOOD MORNING"
This sounds better

but

A happy person will say "GOOD MORNING"
The voice lifts and this greeting has warmth and vitality

MORE THAN A GREETING

The greeting can be uplifting or a great put-down. Whichever it is, the greeting creates the tone of *what's to follow.* If people realized how important the greeting is, they'd take more care when saying it.

A loving greeting is a vital part of contact among friends. A less personal but warm greeting is an expression of goodwill between acquaintances or strangers. We can tell a lot about a person and his state of mind by his greeting.

THE FRIENDLY GREETING

When we go into a shop, a friendly "good morning" makes us feel welcome. An indifferent or bored greeting—if we get one at all—aggravates us. We feel like taking our business somewhere else. Unfortunately, too many retailers treat their customers in this way. They don't seem to appreciate the value of the greeting.

While the greeting is the first verbal signal, body language plays a big part, too. It seems silly to mention the smile as it's so obvious, but how many of us use it effectively? Yet a smile added to a cheery greeting is delightful.

In business, from the executive suite to the factory floor, a surprising amount of friendliness can be generated by the greeting, even if that is the extent of the contact. The chief executive who always has a cordial greeting for the office cleaners will be appreciated, especially if he has taken the trouble to remember their names as well.

HELPING SHYNESS

Young people are often too shy or nervous to use the greeting properly. It's a pity when this happens, for a good greeting gives confidence. Who can resist answering with equal enthusiasm? Once the ice is broken, it's easier to talk naturally. A *grunt* can never take the place of a pleasant greeting. Some think that when you work daily side by side with associates, a morning greeting is not necessary, but those who do greet others with warmth and friendliness know that it generates good feelings.

The voice is the most wonderfully
expressive instrument
in the world

Think of your voice as a

MUSICAL INSTRUMENT

Don't plod along using a

DULL...DULL...DULL...MONOTONE

or the

"ONE-NOTE SAMBA"

OUR MUSICAL INSTRUMENT

Some of you may think that comparing the human voice to a musical instrument is crazy, but the more I think of it, the more convinced I am. The voice has an amazing range, incredible versatility, and is able to convey every possible feeling or emotion. It is to speech what a violin or piano is to music.

To hear the voice used superbly is an experience never to be forgotten. The tragedy is that so few of us use even a fraction of its range. It takes less effort to drone away in a flat, one-note tone. In time we get so used to the sound of our voices we never give it another thought and don't appreciate what they are capable of achieving.

MEMORIES

A distinctive voice creates a memory within us. When we hear the voice again, we react to it in the same way in which a familiar piece of music evokes a memory, even if we haven't heard it for a long time.

Think about your voice as a musical instrument. Think, too, about how often it's abused. Listen to people. Compare their voices to musical instruments. Study the flow of their speech. Try to pick out the sounds that offend your ear as well as those that are pleasant to listen to. Decide if speakers are using anywhere near the full range of their voices.

Imagine yourself listening to an orchestra. One or two instruments are out of tune. What would you do? You'd probably cover your ears to avoid the discordant sounds! It's the same with speech. A musical voice is appreciated, an *out-of-tune* one is not.

MEN, TOO!

And don't be fooled into thinking that only women have musical voices. Some men have wonderfully rich and resonant voices. It's worth putting a little time into improving your voice. Someone in business might say, "I certainly don't need a musical voice!" But take it from me, if you can use your voice so that people listen attentively to you, understand you, and remember your words, you will always have an advantage.

How does speech compare to music?

COMPATIBLE SOUNDS

When we really think about it, we realize how alike speech and music are. Both speech and music are international, regardless of language and tempo. Speech and music bring people closer together. Speech and music are based on the emotions.

The *notes* in music are similiar to the *range* of the voice. We may not have as many actual notes in our voice as a piano, but basically they both go up and down the scale.

THE PIZZAZZ OF JAZZ

In music, we have fortissimo and pianissimo, allegretto and crescendo. In speech, we speak loudly and softly, communicate quickly and briskly, build up the power in our voices. In music, we have waltzes, marches, gavottes. In speech, we can have a lilt to our voice, punch out our words, sound formal and structured. In music, we have jazz and the blues and rock 'n' roll. In speech, we may have a voice that oozes pizzazz or the plaintive sounds of suffering, or perhaps the exuberant calls of youth.

But no matter what the melody, always remember that two musicians may play the same music, but that music can sound completely different. One may have style and professionalism and the other may not. It's the same with speech.

MUSIC PLUS WORDS

When words are added to music, the bonds become even stronger. Looking at the combination from the speech point of view, we can learn a lot.

There is the grand passion of opera, the soft tones of a lullaby, the urgent notes of a patriotic song. We have songs expressing all the joys and desires and hopes of a lover. We may find solace in hymns and spiritual songs.

Whatever the emotion, we can find ways to express it if we listen to both the words and the music, then incorporate the essence of both into our speech.

The easiest way to study speech is to

listen to other people

THE TOOL OF TELEVISION

Listening to other people is something of an art. It's embarrassing if we stare at people, drinking in their every word, so I suggest you use your television. There you can sit as close as you like for as long as you like, taking in every inflection, every emphasis, every pause. You can analyze, judge, or laugh, but most important *you can learn*. What can you learn? Listen to the speakers' delivery. Is it natural? nervous? aggressive? Overall, is their speech monotonous? flat? lively? Is their voice pleasant to listen to? harsh? quiet?

How do the speakers say their words? Is their speech sloppy? Are they mumblers or jabberers? Do they enunciate clearly?

Do they say a lot of "ums" and "ers" or stick in other useless words such as "you know"? At what pace are they speaking? too quickly? too slowly? just right?

THE SOUNDS THEY MAKE

Listen carefully to their *voices*. Are they high pitched, low pitched, or medium pitched? Are there a variety of tones? Do their voices have a quality that you admire or one that makes you want to tune out?

Do they include an upward inflection at the end of sentences?

Can you tell if they're breathing well, or are they taking in gulps of air mid-sentence? Do they say their words with color and conviction?

PRESENTING THEIR CASES

How are they getting information across? Is it clear, or are they confusing you? Do they jump from one subject to another?

Are you able to concentrate or does your mind keep wandering? Are you learning anything from what they're telling you? Is their information coming across in a clear, logical way?

Do they sound confident, or is their anxiety about being on television showing? Train yourself to detect the good and the bad communicators. Teach yourself how to discard the bad aspects from your own speech and include what you admire.

When you can recognize both

FAULTS AND STRENGTHS

in speech

LISTEN

to the way

YOU SOUND

OOOHHH! IS THAT MY VOICE?

Your own voice can be the most awful, horrifying sound in the world! We all shrink from listening to it at first, until we get used to how we sound and can begin to hear it more *objectively.*

This is the key. We've got to get over that initial feeling and use what we hear to help us develop our voice, train our voice, use our voice in a thousand different ways until it begins to have a professional ring to it.

OFF OR ON?

How should we listen to our voices?

Well, there are several ways. The obvious one is by speaking into a tape recorder, but there are problems here. When we try this method, we become tense sitting in front of a microphone. We tend to use strangely garbled language and end up not sounding like ourselves at all. Hearing this played back is intimidating.

Apart from the fact that we aren't speaking well, there's the added problem that microphones are so sensitive they pick up extra sounds we can't always hear.

If you decide to use a tape recorder, try putting one out of sight and then talk about your favorite subject to a friend. Chat between yourselves so that before long you forget the tape recorder's there.

Always *tell people* if you're doing this. I've known more than one instance where a tape recorder has been hidden and there has been hell to pay afterwards. Nobody likes to discover that unguarded conversations and remarks have been recorded.

HEARING YOURSELF

You can, of course, talk to a video camera. But because you want to concentrate on your voice only, it's better to stick to a tape recorder. The more experienced you become, the easier it will be for you to listen to yourself, by yourself. When you can do this, you've hit the jackpot. Being able to assess your own performance and do something to improve it is the mark of the professional.

Why do some people sound better than others?

THERE'S SOUND AND SOUND

Interesting speech is more than just speaking. It's a combination of how we sound, the words we say, and how we put them together. Somewhere in there we can also find the art of selecting the right word and the right word picture.

THAT CERTAIN WORD

If I were to take my finger and very lightly touch the side of a glass a few times what word would describe this action the best? *Tap.* Tap is made up of two aspirate (or breathy) consonants, with a short vowel in between.

If I used my knuckles and made a noise on a door, it's a *knock.* Again two aspirate consonants but this time with a heavier vowel in the middle. If I took my fist and hit a table it would be *thump* or *bang.* Both are heavy sounds in consonants and vowels.

If I used my middle finger and *flicked* it against my thumb I am doing virtually the same motion with my lower lip against my teeth to say the word *flicked.* The word is similiar to the action. If I ran my nails down a blackboard (and I'm sure you shudder at the thought!), the word would be *scratch* or *screech.*

GET THE FEELING

In each case the word sounds like the action, so it's *onomatopoeic.* These are basic words, but we can use the same idea with so many other ones and by the way we say them create the right effect.

If I said, "I'm so tired," it wouldn't be the same as saying, "I'm so t-i-r-e-d." By stretching the vowel, I put the feeling of being tired into the word. Experiment with words. Make some short and snappy, some longer, some soft, others sharp, aggressive, emotional, gentle.

Take words like *exciting, fantastic, ghastly, dreadful, powerful, passionate, awful, wonderful, loving, exasperating, enchanting...* and make the sound convey your meaning as much as the words themselves.

Gabble Gabble Gabble Gabble Gabble Gabble Gabble Gabble Gabble Gabble

SOUND FAMILIAR?

SLOW DOWN!

Ask people what kind of voice irritates them the most and many will include the *gabbling* voice. When a person gabbles, words are poured out so rapidly and indistinctly they're almost impossible to interpret.

Sometimes this is the result of nerves. Most of us speak a little more quickly when we're under pressure, but this can be controlled by practice and perseverance.

It's when *gabbling* becomes the norm that we have to do something drastic about it.

CHICKEN?

It's interesting to look up *gabble* in a dictionary. According to Webster, it means, "to utter inarticulate sounds (as of a chicken)." Appropriate, don't you think?

As with many faults, *gabbling* can only be controlled by strict mental discipline. Nobody but the gabbler can do it. It's very much a do-it-yourself project.

First and foremost, gabblers must discover that they are just that, gabblers. People who have spoken with the speed of a racehorse all their lives may not realize that they have a problem. This is where learning to listen to your voice is such a help.

SLOPPY SPEECH

If you think, or know, you speak too quickly, try to s*low down*. Every time you get the urge to speak rapidly, make yourself *slow down.*

The act of *slowing down* helps you to form your words more carefully. Rapid speech is often combined with poor enunciation. If this is your trouble, you're going to have to take extra care with the way you actually pronounce words.

It may seem like a lot of work. If you think it isn't worth it, just remember that your future could be at stake. An exaggeration? I think not. If people can't *hear* what you say and are irritated by the way you speak, you're putting yourself at a real disadvantage.

A period of self-training may work wonders.

Then there's the

IRRITATING

habit of an

upward inflection

at the **end**

of a

sentence

BREAK THE HABIT

The upward inflection is used naturally when we're asking a *question.* "Why are you doing that?" If we put it into any other part of our speech, it gives our voices an indefinite quality, as though we aren't sure of our facts. In other words, we're making statements sound like questions.

I once heard a young woman say, "My name is June Smith. I live in the city, where I work as a typist." Not only was it dreadful to listen to, but it made her sound like a person who had little faith in her own ability.

NOT UP

This nasty little habit creeps into so much speech, not only at the end of sentences but also at the end of phrases.

If she had spoken in a positive way, saying, "My name is JUNE SMITH. I live in the CITY, where I work as a TYPIST," she would have sounded more confident.

People evaluate us as soon as we start speaking. The upward inflection, which oozes self-doubt, is something that can quickly turn people off when we are speaking.

BE POSITIVE

When you begin to analyze the speech of other people, listen carefully for these upward inflections. Listen, too, to those who do not have them in their speech. Discover how much more authoritative they sound.

When you can pick up the inflections easily, turn your ear inward and make sure you don't have them.

Most people learn to react quickly when they hear themselves use the upward inflection. "I've done it again!" they say, and because they recognize the negative effect it has on their speech, they try very hard to get rid of it.

More thoughts
on that

IRRITATING

upward inflection

QUESTIONING SPEECH

Ask people to name one of the most aggravating habits of speech and many will tell you that it is the upward inflection at the end of a sentence when the sentence is not a question.

AN INTRUSION

Recording your voice can reveal the intrusion of the upward inflection in strange places. Many people say their *names* with a flick up at the end, and they don't even know they're doing it.

I once had a senior executive attend a course who had to say his name eleven times before he got rid of the upward inflection. Three times he said, "My name is John Jones." The others interrupted him. "You're doing it again!" they said. "I know," he said. "I can hear it!" But he kept on doing it, so they began to count—that's how I remember it was eleven—"eight, nine, ten..." On the last try, he said, strongly and positively, "My name is JOHN JONES," and everybody clapped!

WE FIND IT HERE...WE FIND IT THERE...

The upward inflection can be found in the oddest places: in company names, street names, when we're telling stories, giving advice, being polite. Some of the time it's when we're under stress, or perhaps a little nervous.

Some say that it's just how the people in their country speak, whether they're from America, Britain, Canada, Australia, or New Zealand. Nonsense! It's how *poor* speakers in any country talk. It is not how *good* speakers talk.

Watch any game show on television. The host asks a contestant, "What's the capital of England?" If the reply is "London" what are they telling us? They're not sure. If they say "LONDON" in a firm and positive way it sounds as though they know the right answer.

So, if you suspect you're adding this less-than-colorful habit to your speech, the only advice is to *get rid of it* any way you can.

I've often heard it said that if you have
ENTHUSIASM
you don't need anything else

I DON'T BELIEVE THAT

You must always have enthusiasm

but it needs to be
DISCIPLINED ENTHUSIASM

Have you ever listened to an *enthusiastic amateur*
who *babbles* away
and you can't understand a word?

MADLY E-N-T-H-U-S-I-A-S-T-I-C!

Speech really can become babble at times. We only have to ask an enthusiastic amateur speaker what a film was like and he's off!

"Oh, it was *wonderful!* This happened and then that happened...but before that happened something else happened. And she did this and he did that...or was it the other way around?"

The speaker's inability to tell the story in a clear, logical way ends up *confusing* you.

MISINTERPRETATION

This can happen in business too. There are many people who cannot express themselves well, and this often leads to *mis*interpretation.

The skills of communicators involve more than the way we *speak*. They include how we put words together, how we use and choose language, how we select the words to speak and toss out those more suited to written language.

THE WAY TO THINK

How we think is extremely important. If we present our thoughts all jumbled up and out of sequence how can we expect our listeners to get the right picture? I have an easy way to help people create a simple, easy-to-follow plan that is ideal for speakers, writers, and thinkers.

Memory trees are excellent for some types of work, but they can be complicated and hard to take in at a glance. My plan is just the opposite. It gives detailed information in seconds. (See page 118.)

The main thing is not to fall into the trap of amateur enthusiasm. Don't get so carried away that you can't cope with the rush of thoughts and words that flow from you. When this happens, pity the poor listeners!

We can still show our enthusiasm in a more controlled and fluent fashion without lessening the effect.

POINT TO PONDER

how can we
become
FLUENT
speakers?

MENTAL DISCIPLINE

Most of us know what we want to say. The difficulty is in actually saying it and saying it in a way that persuades people to listen. The breakdown often occurs somewhere between our brains and our mouths!

There is a reasonably simple way of correcting this, but you have to work at it. The answer is to start speaking all the time *when you're alone.* Do it in the bath or shower, while you're driving, or mowing the lawn.

This speech should not be your usual chatter or business talk. It has to be on specific subjects, subjects you give yourself.

PRACTICE, PRACTICE

You say, "Today, I'm going to speak about soil." And you do. You build up your talk, category by category, and you speak it *out loud.* When you've finished with soil, you might talk about trains, jellyfish, curtains, or photographs. Choose easy subjects at first, then, as you progress, try harder ones—jealousy, family relationships, business management, leadership.

To begin with, you might talk about each subject for about 30 seconds, but as you keep changing subjects and get more proficient, you'll be able to stretch your speeches to whatever length you want. The secret lies in your ability to instantly turn...

YOUR THOUGHTS INTO ACTION

The effort you put into this will reward you many, many times over. What you're doing is training yourself to be able to speak *on any subject at any time.* This has enormous spin-offs in life in general, but it is especially useful in business.

However, you must do more than just talk. It's imperative to employ all the skills we talk about in this book: pitch and pace, vary the pause, use colors, and add vitality. Each time you practice, set a goal. *Start* your subject and *finish* your subject, even if it only lasts half a minute. Trailing off into nothing will not give you the satisfaction of producing a whole speech. The more you do it, the better you'll get!

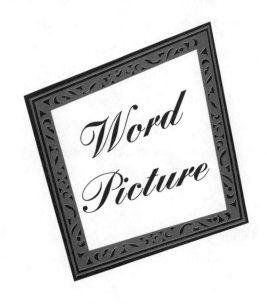

Word Picture

A contradiction in terms?

What does it mean?

How does it apply to speech?

How do we DO it?

Why SHOULD we do it?

PAINTING THE PICTURE

Communication must be two-way. When we give information there has to be feedback. If there isn't feedback there's a breakdown somewhere. Our audience should be able to "see" everything we say from our perspective. In other words, we must speak in "word pictures" or paint a verbal picture.

Years ago, in Britain, when archaeology was regarded as a musty old subject, there burst onto the television screen a tall, fine-looking man with a large handle-bar moustache. He was Professor Wheeler, later Sir Mortimer Wheeler. He had a passion for archaeology and he was also a brilliant communicator. When he spoke about archaeology, people saw it all through his eyes and with his enthusiasm.

NOT JUST A POT

He would hold up little broken pots or vases, explain what they were made of, and who made them, what sort of lives those people led: their loves, their hates, their wars, their civilization, and the breakdown of their civilization. He did it with such love that viewers were riveted.

It was as though they had stepped back in time, and archaeology was for them never the same again. That's what I mean by *word pictures*. Being able to create them is vital to our success. Sometimes people complain that it's all very well for someone with an exciting life, but their lives are so dull and uneventful there is nothing to get inspired or enthusiastic about.

THE PASSION

Then I tell them about a friend of mine. He makes wire rope. Now if you can think of anything more mundane than that I'll give you a medal! Yet when he talks about it he has the same passion for wire rope that Professor Wheeler had for archaeology. He loves everything about it—its strength, its durability, and its versatility—and when he speaks, I see it through his eyes. I'll never think of wire rope as just wire rope again. If someone can do such a remarkable job when talking about wire rope just think what you can do with your subject.

To discover how good

—or bad—we are

we have only to

HEAR

ourselves through the

ears of children

WINNIE-THE-POOH

Once, in a training session, a man came to me and said, "Marie, why is it that when I read to my children—they're three and five—they run away to play?"

"Well," I said, "you mustn't be doing it very well! Next time you come, bring a book."

So he did. He came with *Winnie-the-Pooh* by A. A. Milne under his arm. Now *Winnie-the-Pooh* is superb reading, with so many adventures and imagery. Also, it has great characters, including Winnie-the-Pooh, Eeyore, and Owl. "Use your voice," I said, "and get plenty of variety into it. There are not only many wonderful words to emphasize and little dramas to make exciting, but there are also the different voices of each character."

A MORAL

When he came again, I asked how he did. He laughed and said, "I can't believe it, they won't let me stop." Now there's a moral to this little tale. Children as young as three and five knew *instinctively* when Dad was being dead boring! But when Dad improved, they couldn't get enough.

When adults listen to a dreary speaker, they can't run away to play. They *tune out.* Even if they want to listen, dullness in a speaker's voice keeps them tuning in and out, and in doing so they could be missing some important information. With the best will in the world they can't concentrate fully, and the *speaker* is the one at a disadvantage.

GET THE FEELING

In business, as elsewhere, *every word counts.* Every word must be absorbed by the listener. You can usually tell if information is being processed. If you're making a speech and your audience becomes restless, inattentive, and moves a lot they're trying to tell you something. It could be that you're boring the socks off them. If a glazed look comes over the person sitting opposite you in an office, if she sighs or glances surreptitiously at her watch that's a sign for *you* to watch it!

Listen carefully to how you

PRONOUNCE

your words

They're not always

said the way

you think

WORDS, WORDS, WORDS

We get confused, sometimes even embarrassed, when people *mispronounce* words. Mostly, mispronunciation arises because speakers aren't aware of the way words should sound. But often the people they're talking to are judging them as they speak, evaluating their education or lack of it, not to mention their *professionalism.*

Poor pronunciation, combined with generally sloppy speech, may give the impression that a person is not qualified for a particular job, even before other skills are discovered.

UNDERSTOOD?

I've heard it said that it doesn't matter *how* you say your words so long as you're *understood.* In some ways I agree with that, but it's true only to a point. And the point *is* that frequently listeners *do not understand* badly pronounced words or sloppy speech.

So what happens? Speakers have to repeat themselves. By repeating themselves, they're on the defensive. And if this happens a lot it can affect their confidence.

THE DICTIONARY

The obvious place to check how to pronounce a word is in a dictionary. The only trouble is that the pronunciation is presented in phonetics, and is not always easy to work out.

An easier way is to listen to how other people pronounce words, especially good speakers. Listen to the radio and the television too. What you'll hear won't always be perfect, but it will certainly get you off to a good start. If you're still not sure how to pronounce specific words, ask. Just make sure you ask the right person!

It doesn't matter if you make mistakes now and again so long as you keep progressing overall. The main thing is not to get stuck in a rut.

NOUNS

PRONOUNS

ADJECTIVES

ADVERBS

SINGULAR   VERBS

PLURAL   PREPOSITIONS

GENDER   CONJUNCTIONS

GERUND

POSSESSIVE

SYNTAX   OBJECTIVE

SPLIT INFINITIVES

DANGLING MODIFIERS

AGREEMENT

INTERJECTIONS

DOES GRAMMAR MATTER?

KNOW YOUR BASICS

Yes. Grammar *does* matter, but not to the point where we're going to panic over it. The mere mention of the word *grammar* sends some people into a spin. Yet in most cases they're doing nearly everything right anyway. The purists may not agree, but I think that we can become pedantic about the subject if we're not careful.

The more we know about grammar the better. It is relatively simple and logical, and isn't as frightening as we sometimes imagine it to be.

UNCOUTH?!

With written language, we have to be careful because mistakes jump right off the page and hit us. The spoken word is easier because it's accepted that sometimes we do speak *un*grammatically. However, there are some points of grammar that can make us appear uncouth if we get them wrong.

We all get a bit muddled sometimes and wonder if we've got our pronouns right or have mixed up our tenses. At the same time, we tend to judge other people by the way they handle their grammar.

Here are some annoying mistakes: "Him and me..." instead of "He and I..."; "I was laying down having a rest..." rather than "I was lying down..."; and "He did good on his exam..." instead of "He did well..."

BUY A BOOK

Grammar is just one more aspect of speech that we need to be careful of, especially when we're in the company of people who speak English well. Notice, too, how others speak. Learn to detect poor grammar, then vow never to make such mistakes! If you're not sure what to do yourself, buy a book on grammar and study it. There are far too many points to mention here, but I think it is important that we become aware of the part grammar plays in our overall pattern of speech.

The more you increase your word power and understand the structure of your language the easier it will be to make a good impression.

Some aspects of

SPEECH

we can DEFINITELY do

WITHOUT

PITFALLS

Speech is peppered with pitfalls. Even one of these can make us seem amateurish, so it's important that we are aware of them and that we get rid of them. I'm sure you've heard of them all, but how often do they slip into your speech without you realizing it?

The most obvious pitfall is the *cliché*. The cliché is hackneyed, tired, second-hand language. There was an old cliché joke that said, "Avoid clichés like the plague!" Clichés are phrases like "tongue-in-cheek," "bored to tears," "it's got to get worse before it gets better," "leave no stone unturned," "a bee in your bonnet," "take someone down a peg or two," "let's get down to brass tacks," "not my cup of tea"—the list is endless. Always try for an original turn of a phrase, or at least one that doesn't fall into the cliché trap.

A *tautology* is one of my pet peeves. From the Greek word *tautos,* meaning "same," a tautology is the use of two words where one would do. People talk about "no other alternative," but *other* isn't needed because *alternative* means just that. In "to merge together" *together* isn't needed. You might say "the general consensus," but the word *general* isn't needed. *Consensus* means "general agreement." "At the present time" means simply "now." Here, too, the list goes on and on.

Euphemisms are silly, inoffensive little words or phrases used as substitutes for stronger, perhaps hurtful ones. How often have you heard someone talk about the "dear departed" or "going to the little girls' room"? Advertisers make the most of euphemisms when they speak about "the fuller figure" instead of "large," or "economy goods" when they mean "cheap." During a war the most ridiculous statements include euphemisms: "the final solution" means "death"; "logistical strikes" usually mean "bombing raids." Politicians are notorious for their euphemistic statements, such as "frank discussions."

Speech needs to be fresh and lively, not jaded and tired.

IT'S

NERVE-RACKING

WHEN YOU DON'T HAVE

THE **RIGHT** WORD

AT THE **RIGHT** MOMENT

HAVING WORDS ON TAP

The fear of not being able to come out with the right word at the right moment discourages a lot of people from speaking up. Being able to think of the right words and use them is essential for anyone who has aspirations as a speaker at any level.

If you haven't a natural ability to let words flow, then you'll have to train yourself. *Practice.* It's not difficult, but it takes perseverance.

We've talked about choosing a word, any word, and speaking about it out loud to yourself. (See page 51.) That's a great help. Using a moon chart (see page 122), you can select a topic, fill in the categories, and talk to yourself out loud. This is to familiarize yourself with ordinary, everyday subjects so that you have all the right words on tap.

BOOKS, BOOKS, BOOKS

Buy books on words. I'm constantly buying books about language. I love them, read them like novels, and always learn something new. Right word, wrong word, grammar, elements of style, English usage, usage and abusage, plain words, language and linguistics... I don't always do what I'm told, but I do gain a lot from them.

I treasure my dictionaries. I have several, including a poet's manual and rhyming dictionary, which is fun. Books help you realize the incredible range of words available to you.

THE THESAURUS

If I had to live on a desert island with only one book, I'd chose a thesaurus. I have six and they are in constant use. My favorite would be the famous *Roget's Thesaurus.* I keep it near me all the time, checking on shades of meaning, alternative words, degrees of emotion, and varieties of expression. It's called a "storehouse of the English language" and it is just that. I spend hours browsing through it, savoring the diversity and richness of words of all kinds: formal, informal, colloquial, poetic. If you don't own any of these books yet, go to your local library or book shop and look at what they have before you buy.

WE TALK ABOUT A

Beautiful scene
        Beautiful car
Beautiful flower
      Beautiful picture
Beautiful woman
      Beautiful garden
Beautiful dress
       Beautiful baby
Beautiful tree
       Beautiful day
Beautiful show
      Beautiful food
Beautiful room
       Beautiful city
Beautiful wedding
     Beautiful kitchen
Beautiful gift
      Beautiful country
Beautiful design
      Beautiful ring
Beautiful ship
     Beautiful harbor
Beautiful face

BUT WHAT DO WE MEAN EXACTLY?

THE "BEAUTIFUL" SYNDROME

The word *beautiful* is subjective. What we might call beautiful, others may not. So in choosing such a word, we're restricting our listeners in their quest to understand what we're telling them.

If you look up *beauty* in a thesaurus, here are a few of the many words you'll find: lovely, good-looking, adorable, majestic, divine, fair, radiant, photogenic, picturesque, graceful, attractive, charming, elegant, captivating, enchanting, dainty, delicate, exquisite, delightful, regal, striking, stunning, chic, glittering, proud, dignified, refined, fascinating, captivating, splendid.

A "WHAT" WOMAN?

Take one word from the list on the previous page, say *woman*. The images conjured up by these words help to fine-tune the description of a particular woman. She could be a pretty woman, a dignified woman, a proud woman, an elegant woman, a charming woman, a dainty woman, a graceful woman. These words all paint a different picture.

Go down the list and try to find a more descriptive adjective for each noun, one that would give your listeners a clearer idea of what you are describing.

I'm not suggesting that you stop using the word *beautiful*, but rather that you try combining it with other, more descriptive words so that you paint a genuinely colorful image.

OVERWORKED "WONDERFUL"

Wonderful is another overworked word. I once heard a television personality use it eight times within a minute and a half when he was introducing a beauty pageant. Everything was "wonderful." It was "wonderful to be with you." "What a wonderful audience!" "The girls are wonderful." "Their clothes are wonderful," and so on. What a bore! *Nice* is another much overworked word to be wary of.

We may notice when other speakers use words like these, but do we realize how much *we* use them?

If I had to sum up

exciting

interesting

dynamic

speech

in one word

I'd say that

the special ingredient

is

VITALITY

VITALITY PLUS

Vitality—I love that word. I couldn't count the times I've stamped my foot and shouted, "Get some *vitality* into it!"

It's a word that encompasses everything that's great in speech: energy, vigor, power, intensity, animation, verve, vivaciousness, sparkle, liveliness, exuberance, zing.

I've seen many people go through some kind of metamorphosis when they discover vitality. It's like a release, a chance to be oneself without fear of failure.

SPIN-OFFS

When people gain vitality it affects more than their voices. All kinds of amazing things happen. They look better and stand taller, and they have courage—they do things they would never have thought possible before. Sometimes they even dress better too. It's surprising how we are able to look at ourselves more objectively when our self-esteem shoots up.

But vitality is not a quality that hides itself so that only the fortunate can find it. It's there waiting. Waiting for everyone. Waiting for you.

THE BIG QUESTION

The question is "How do we get it?" The answer is different for each one of us. Some find it by listening carefully to the way they sound. When they hear themselves sounding *flat* they stop, then speak again with more *vitality*. Others practice *words, phrases,* and *reading aloud.* This helps them discover where they're going wrong.

Overall, we need to learn to transfer that same vitality we have in our *comfort zone*—our homes or with our friends—to the big, wide world around us.

It's so important not to be frightened of standing up for ourselves, of speaking out, of making an impression. Injecting vitality into the way we speak and express ourselves plays an enormous part in transforming us from timid souls into confident people who can be ourselves and do our best *all the time.*

POINT TO PONDER

how can we
become
DYNAMIC
speakers?

MORE WORK!

I have a special exercise for helping people become dynamic speakers. It really is a lot of fun. It makes them use their imaginations as well as their speaking skills.

I give them subjects that are sets of opposites. They have to think not only of what they're going to say, but how they're going to say it. Their choice of words must be exactly right for the subject, but so too must be the way they speak them.

The first subject is *war*. Before they begin, we talk over the type of voice they'll use. It has to be strong, almost heavy, nothing light or frivolous. Then we choose the words that will be used—anguish, fear, disaster, blood, suffering, killing.

The next subject is *peace*. The voice must reflect this new subject, and the words might include tranquillity, harmony, freedom, stillness, silence, serenity.

Then we go to *industry*, and a different voice again. Not as harsh as *war*, but certainly not like *peace*. There has to be activity, machines going bang-bang-bang, noise, energy, constant movement. The words can be short, sharp and fast, like the subject itself.

The fourth one is *leisure*. Ahhhh! Everyone's perception of leisure is different, but the voice is always relaxed and happy. Some use busy descriptions and words like skiing, surfing, running, and walking. Others just flop and we hear words like sun, sand, sea, sleep.

Then we go into emotions, starting with *hate*. That gets them going! The voices are filled with emotion and the words tumble out according to what they really hate.

When we come to *love,* everything about people changes. There's no denying the power of love, and when it's spoken about sincerely and reverently, people look and sound different. Their faces become softer, their eyes glitter, their words reflect their feelings, and tenderness is paramount.

Often the results of this exercise are startling. The word pictures are incredible and people who have never spoken like this publicly before find a release that affects everything else they do. Make a list of your own—and keep going.

Our eyes may be the mirror of the soul

but

SPEECH IS OUR WINDOW TO THE WORLD

Through that window people see many things

They can sense our...

moods

thoughts

hopes

desires

passions

anxiety

confidence

insecurity

knowledge

education

experience

sensitivity

insensitivity

enthusiasm

personality

sexuality

stability

and that's only the beginning!

LOOKING IN

It's a bit spooky, isn't it? The thought that others can form opinions of us in so many ways. Yet we do the same to them. We go to a party and are introduced to someone new. What do we do? Instinctively we look first at their visual image; the type of person they are, their looks, what they're wearing, the quality of their clothes, their colors, how they're groomed, and their posture.

Then they *speak,* and a whole raft of different impressions are let loose. If we don't like what we see and hear, we may move away; if we do, we move closer.

IN OR OUT

This calculated study—whether we're aware of it or not—happens everywhere and to everyone. In business it could mean the difference between getting a job or being passed over. Outside of business too it has a profound effect on our lives. Like most aspects of life, we can do something to help ourselves create a good image. It's not always easy and it may take a lot of work and practice, but it can be done.

I believe in protecting ourselves. We protect ourselves by having confidence. We protect ourselves by speaking authoritatively. We protect ourselves by being able to handle the unexpected. We protect ourselves by always having fluent speech on the tip of our tongue. We protect ourselves by the way we walk, our use of eye contact, and our use of speech.

AT SCHOOL

I can't stress strongly enough that the sooner we learn these language and speaking skills the better chance we have in life. In fact, we should have most of them firmly under our belts before we leave school.

The number of times that people in senior management have said to me, "Why didn't I learn all this at school?" is amazing. And while it's never too late to begin, it's still great to have a head start.

Why are some people more

POPULAR

than others?

LISTENING SKILLS

It seems an obvious thing to say, but how we *listen* to others can have a dramatic effect on our popularity.

We all recognize those who do *not* listen. They seem insensitive, lacking in the warmth we expect from our friends. They annoy us because what we say to them seems to be flying in one ear and out the other.

Even in business, the ability to *listen* is vital to success. A boss who doesn't listen will not get the best out of an employee. A colleague who doesn't listen will not contribute the right qualities to your association. A client who doesn't listen will be unaware of what you're telling them.

WHAT ABOUT YOU?

On the other hand, how well do *you* listen?

Do you wonder sometimes why people don't talk to you much or even avoid you? Could it be that you're always so busy talking *at* them that you never take the time to sit back and listen *to* them?

Listening demands considerable concentration, the ability to put your own thoughts on hold for a time, a high degree of caring, and the skill to make a contribution to the conversation even when you're not saying much.

In other words, you can't fake an interest. It has to be real, even if there are degrees of interest. Obviously, if someone's telling you a juicy piece of gossip, your interest is intense, whereas it may not be quite so focused if you're listening to friends telling you about their travels. But either way, your listening skills should be at work.

BODY LANGUAGE

Naturally, body language plays its part. How you sit, tilt or nod your head, smile or frown, laugh or look concerned—all these and many more are instinctive parts of the listening process. But in every case it has to be genuine to be appreciated.

READING ALOUD
lets you get used to the

SOUND

of
your OWN voice

PUTTING THE SYMBOLS IN

An excellent way to improve your voice is to read aloud. It's surprising how quickly we learn to tune in to the way we sound when we do this regularly. This practice is good, but at the same time we must learn how to use our voices effectively and expressively.

I have three simple symbols that will help you to do just that.

Underline the words you want to *emphasize*

Use a *vertical line* / to denote a *pause*

Add this symbol ∧ when you want your voice to go *up and down* on one word

The first time you read a paragraph, it may sound flat and uninteresting. So put the *symbols* in to bring out the meaning and give it greater vitality. Sometimes you may need two of them for one word. *Read the paragraph aloud again.* This time it may sound somewhat jerky, but *read it aloud again* and *again* until the pauses are what I call flowing pauses. In this way, the paragraph will come to life in a smooth and vital way.

READ THIS PARAGRAPH ALOUD

One of the greatest assets anyone can have is vitality. It makes a tremendous difference to your appearance. Your face becomes more alive and interesting, your eyes shine. It even affects the way you walk. Vitality shows up in your voice too. It gives warmth and enthusiasm—two qualities that attract attention immediately.

NOW PUT THE SYMBOLS IN

One of the greatest ∧assets / ∧anyone can have / ∧is ∧vitality. It makes a tremendous ∧difference / to your ∧appearance. / Your ∧face / becomes / more ∧alive and ∧interesting, / your ∧eyes / shine, it even ∧affects / the ∧way / you ∧walk. / ∧Vitality shows up / in your ∧voice / too. / It gives / ∧warmth and ∧enthusiasm—two ∧qualities / that ∧attract / attention ∧immediately.

PRACTICE

reading aloud

WITH THE

SYMBOLS

IN

NEWSPAPERS

AND YOU'LL

DISCOVER

HOW

EXPRESSIVE

YOU CAN BE!

USE THE NEWSPAPER

To practice reading aloud, there's nothing handier than the newspaper. Written language is not the same as the spoken word, but for sheer convenience, the paper's fine. It gives you a constant stream of articles to read out loud and a variety of themes needing different tones and emotions. It also offers an opportunity to test your ability to use pitch, pace, and pause.

Best of all, you can *mark it!* When you've finished, you can throw it away. You can't do that with your good books and expensive magazines.

A BIT DISJOINTED

Also, it's surprising how *anything* can sound better when you've put in your symbols for emphasis, compound inflections, and the mighty pause.

Try this. Read a piece from a newspaper out loud without marking it. It may sound rather flat, a little disjointed, or hurried.

Go over it again. This time, *put in the symbols.* In every sentence, go for the *sense.* It's surprising how often words come out that don't mean much until exactly the right emphasis is applied and the article is broken down into easy-to-read components. Read it aloud again. Make adjustments to the symbols. Read it aloud again and again, until you feel happy with it.

PERSEVERE

There are two problems with a newspaper: the type is small and the lines are close together. When you've finished marking it, it may be rather difficult to read, but persevere. It can be done.

One short paragraph prepared and read *aloud* daily does help you to get used to the sound of your own voice. It also makes you aware, in a visual way, of how complex good speech can be. You also become aware of how even a few words can have tremendous power.

Think of

COMMUNICATION
THROUGH SPEECH

as being in
3 categories

Knowledge
Interpretation
Technique

TAKING A CLOSER LOOK

We've been told that up to 70 percent of communication can be nonverbal. I find that hard to believe, although I do know that a lot of it is nonverbal. But how would we communicate *properly* if we could use only our body language? Not very well, I suspect.

No, I'm afraid there is no substitute for it. We have to speak in order to communicate. So we might as well do it to the best of our ability.

This subject has been uppermost in my mind for a long time now. I like to offer people an opportunity to learn about speech in the easiest possible way. If we take everything down to the lowest common denominator we find that speech divides easily into three main categories.

DIFFERENT SOUNDS

Before we go into the three categories in more detail, let's think about sound. There is the sound we hear as we speak. There is also the same sound as heard by other people. They are never the same! That's one reason why we're always so surprised to hear a recording of our voices. It's seldom as we expect it to be.

The study of the actual sounds of language is known as phonetics. Look at any book on phonetics and the chances are you won't get far, as it's a detailed and complicated subject. In the following pages, I've tried to simplify the structure of sound and how best to produce it.

ENERGY

To be able to communicate well, you need an important ingredient: energy. It's not quite the same energy as in push-ups or running a marathon, but rather it's a vocal energy that makes sure you are audible.

The required energy differs according to the occasion, of course. You don't need nearly as much energy to have a chatty conversation on the telephone as you do to address a large audience. Yet, even with the telephone conversation, there has to be enough energy to be heard. The experienced speaker always has a store of energy in reserve.

Now to the categories...

First there's our

KNOWLEDGE

Everybody
in the world
has a
UNIQUE blend of
knowledge

KNOWLEDGE AND WHERE IT COMES FROM

We tend to think of knowledge as education, but that's only one segment of it. Academic qualifications, important though they may be, play a relatively small part.

The rest of our knowledge accumulates from the time of our birth, so family, background, and activities within the home are important. Our involvement with society in its many guises gives us a never-ending supply of knowledge.

So do all the interests and hobbies we have, from sports to reading, art to mechanics, television and radio to films and theater. Any form of training adds to it, as does everything within the business arena, and so it goes on *ad infinitum*. The great thing is that no two people have exactly the same *blend of knowledge*.

ALL YOU NEED?

Some people feel that if you have a lot of knowledge that's all you need. I don't altogether agree. Unless that knowledge is able to be *communicated*, it's locked up inside and not productive enough.

We only have to go to any school, technical institute, or university to see students going to sleep in class because they are not being inspired.

Sometimes a person, perhaps with little academic qualifications, has this ability to inspire, persuade, cajole, capture the imagination—and it makes all the difference!

When great knowledge and the ability to communicate are combined in one person, what a treasure we have.

UNIQUE

Because everyone's knowledge is unique, it often saddens me to hear people, young and old, putting themselves down, as though their enormous stores of knowledge were nothing special. They give the impression that they are worthless and have nothing to offer. What nonsense! Some people with even limited stores of knowledge do incredibly well. They make the most of it, and what they don't know they quickly learn. So, it all depends on what we *do* with what we've *got*.

The second category is the

INTERPRETATION

of knowledge

If a speaker's voice is

DULL, DREARY, FLAT, TEDIOUS, HUMDRUM

SINGSONG, COLORLESS, TONELESS, BORING

OR M-O-N-O-T-O-N-O-U-S

We only listen for a few minutes then tune out

We have to do better than that!

THE WAY WE SAY IT

It's all very well having exciting words and phrases in our *heads*. Yet it's how they come out that's important. This is what is going to make for either heavy, plodding speech or fascinating, scintillating talk.

I exaggerate of course! We don't have to be scintillating all the time, but we do need to be able to hold our listeners' attention. When we hear people with lively, interesting voices we sit up and take notice.

WHAT DO THEY DO?

They use a variety of tones and inflections. They vary their pace. They use plenty of pauses.

They also take words and twist them, punch them, s-t-r-e-t-c-h them, tickle them, calm them, *love* them.

In other words, they use language as a living, breathing, exhilarating experience rather than producing stiff, formal, precise, grammatical statements.

I keep saying that we have to listen. And we do. We have to get a *feeling* for language. We get this by becoming so familiar with the way people speak that it's second nature to take it all in.

It doesn't matter whether they're good or bad or just indifferent. We can learn a lot from poor speakers because they show us the way we *shouldn't* speak.

VIDEO TRUTHS

We can also absorb an enormous amount by simply sitting in front of our television sets and analyzing the brilliance of a quality speaker.

When people watch themselves in video playback, they are often appalled to see that what they thought was going to be good speech is, in fact, flat and uninteresting.

So to be able to interpret speech in a professional manner, it's vital that we study all types of speech, from as many quarters as possible. Only then can we make a reasonable judgment about ourselves.

To **INTERPRET** really well

think of the

SIX Ps

Pitch

Pace

Pause

Power

Passion

Professionalism

EASY TO REMEMBER

I like the six Ps. They're easy to remember.

I could have called *pitch* "tone." I could have called *pace* "speed."

But there's no finer word for pause than *pause*.

And as for the next two, what could be more suitable than *power* and *passion*?

They say it all. Together they form an avalanche of meaning, strength, imagination, and bright, swirling color.

Professionalism? It has to be there. It's the level we should all work towards, because if we don't, then all our efforts are for naught.

WHO IS AND WHO ISN'T

After a while, you know instinctively who is professional and who isn't.

When they're not professional, they haven't quite mastered the other Ps.

When they are professional, they've got the other five Ps working for them full time. They'll know it and so will you.

But knowing and doing are not the same thing. It's great to be able to recognize excellence. It's imperative that you aim for nothing less.

REPEAT AND REPEAT

Repeat certain words or phrases again and again. Explore different ways of saying them. Study the pitch, the pace, the pause, and discover how and why they make such a difference to your voice.

It's the trial and error that helps you establish your method of interpretation. This is the path to professionalism.

Sometimes it's a lift of the voice in the middle of a word. Sometimes it's slowing down and punching out your sentences. It may be that you're speaking too quickly. Possibly your voice is too high and you sound childish. Whatever the problem is, it can be improved.

Let's start with

PITCH

the sound we hear

To be interesting, that sound
has to have
VARIETY

VARIETY OF PITCH

Do you vary your vocal pitch? A dictionary defines *pitch* as "the relative sound of a note; the degree of highness and lowness of tone." So think of the voice as having three main registers: low, middle, and high.

If you saw a graph of a dull speaker, it would be a fairly tight band of sound, including the middle range, a little of the top range and a little of the bottom register. If we speak this way all the time the result is a dreary monotone. What the children call "b-o-r-i-n-g!"

If you saw the same graph of an interesting, exciting speaker, it would use the whole of the three main registers all the time.

FROM HIGH TO LOW

The middle range is straightforward and we use it constantly. The top register is what I call the "light and shade" of speech. This is needed to put life and vitality into what we say. The flat version is uninteresting, but when the voice lifts in the middle of a word, it takes on a different feeling.

We use the higher range to convey meaning in all sorts of ways. Say the phrases "It was so exciting!"; "The show was fantastic!"; "I love it!"; "Oh! It was dreadful!"; "What a wonderful view!" If these were said in a flat voice, each one would not convey our real meaning; but add a flick into the upper register on the main words and suddenly our speech has much more expression. It gives our listeners a sense of how we feel.

THE AUTHORITY

However, if we spoke only in the middle to high registers all the time, we would sound childish. We need the lower range and deeper notes for *authority*. It's surprising how we react when we hear that note of authority in people's voices. We assume they know what they're talking about. It's essential to sound authoritative, whether we're selling, buying, giving orders, speaking on the telephone, making a speech, or talking to our children.

You must also bring variety of

PACE

into your speaking

By *quickening* the **un**important words and phrases,
you *slow down* and really *punch out* the *important ones*

Listen to top professional speakers
You'll find that their speech is lively and interesting with plenty of

COLOR AND TONAL VARIETY

Their voices RISE and
FALL

They constantly change pace

This gives strength to speech

THE IMPORTANCE OF PACE

A lot of people can recognize the *monotony* of *pitch*, but very few people realize that the professional speaker also changes *pace* constantly.

If you listen to the average speaker, he goes on and on at the same speed. Even if he varies his pitch, the speech will be boring because of the monotonous pace. But professionals *play with pace.* They quicken the unimportant words and phrases (we can pick those up easily), then they slow down and hammer out the important ones. *Bang. Bang. Bang.* Then they speed up again. It's like the way they used to teach the fox-trot: SLOW - SLOW - QUICK - QUICK - SLOW.

CONSTANT CHANGE

Speech is like that too. There should be *constant change.* When change of pace is combined with change of pitch, the audience is never sure what's coming next, because there's no predictability about it. They *have* to listen. The minute predictability creeps into our speech, we've lost them. Even if we lose them only partially, that's still a loss.

Pace adds real *excitement* to our speech. It's the "on again, off again" that strikes the dreary all-the-same pattern a blow!

When you really start listening to others, make *pace* one of your objectives. How does that person handle pace? If she's speaking all the time at the same speed, is that one of the reasons you can't concentrate on what she's saying?

THE SECRET

When you find a stimulating speaker, take special note once again of his pace. Listen to how he slows down and punches out the important words, and how he speeds up and rolls away the unimportant phrases. His words always come out at a different rate. That's the *secret.*

When you concentrate on including a change of pace in your own speech, it will probably feel a little strange at first, but as with anything that will improve your speech, *keep at it.* Keeping at it is the only way you're going to succeed. After a while, it will come naturally and you won't even be aware of it.

Let's say you're

SPEAKING WELL

when

suddenly a

PAUSE

looms

What do you do?

APPLAUSE FOR A PAUSE

Apart from pitch and pace, I'd say that the ability to use the *pause* effectively is the big difference between the amateur and the professional speaker. Why do I say this? Because pausing shows that (a) the speaker is confident enough to pause without feeling silly, (b) her language has style, and (c) she's discovered a wonderful world where speech can become magic.

THE PANIC BUTTON

An amateur speaker may be going along nicely, when suddenly a pause looms.

The tendency is to *panic.* Good grief, they think, a pause! I've got to fill it. And what do they fill it with? Yes, of course, they nervously shove in "ums" and "ers," "ahs" and "ehs," "you know," "sort of," "kind of," "and-um, and-a," anything but a *pause.* They're terrified of silence.

But a professional loves the pause, plays with the pause. A single sentence might have four, six, a dozen maybe. Not great gaping holes in speech, just slight ones, some almost infinitesimal. Occasionally the pauses are so tiny that you may not even be aware that they're there, unless you know what to listen for. Yet this is one of the strengths of speech.

If you want to emphasize a word, you pause before it, then really punch out the word. If you want to make your word stand out even more, you pause before it, punch out the word, and pause again after it. This is equivalent to putting your word in bold type.

LEGAL

Lawyers know that you can change the legal meaning of a sentence by putting the comma in a different place. The *pause* can also change the sense of a sentence, so it is a potent tool.

Try using the pause yourself. Experiment: put it before important words, and before and after the ones you really want people to remember.

Develop a taste for the pause!

IF YOU WANT TO BE

the leader of a group

at the top of your profession

able to speak out

leave a lasting impression

on

everyone you meet

you must be

aware of

THE POWER OF SPEECH

OUR GREATEST ASSET

At no other time has the word *communication* been heard so often, yet the ability to communicate through speech is often ignored. It never fails to amaze me that so many companies and organizations—local, national, and international—are unaware of the power of speech. Much time, effort, and money goes into the corporate logo, advertising, public relations, and training of all kinds, but quality of speech among executives, employees, and office holders is seldom a priority.

Every time company staff—from the managing director to the receptionist—talks to the public or to clients, they are presenting the image of their company.

TRADITIONAL?

I've heard it said that examining speech is a traditional or old-fashioned way of looking at communication when there are so many forms of visuals and technology available to aid speakers. But when it comes down to the nitty-gritty we have to rely on our own performance. For instance, what good are visuals if we have to give a radio interview? We've got to have the power of speech within us all the time, whether we're in business, job hunting, teaching, bringing up children, representing our city or society.

To gain the power, we have to be aware, first, of our need. Next, we have to have the determination to fulfill that need. Finally, we must have the staying power to make sure that we are not only good at how we speak and communicate, but are prepared to discover more about it as each day goes by, because we never stop learning.

POSSESSING THE POWER

The power of speech makes us stand out from the crowd.

The power of speech gives us confidence.

The power of speech encourages opportunities.

The power of speech gives us the freedom to be ourselves.

The power of speech helps us succeed.

The power of speech draws people to us.

The power of speech helps us persuade...convince...sell.

PASSION

PASSION

PASSION

PASSION

PASSION

Which degree of
PASSION

applies to your speech?

BURSTING THROUGH

Just as the size of the word *passion* on the previous page changed—starting small and gradually building up—so does our ability to speak passionately about our subjects.

I say to people, "*Language* is my *passion*!" They know, by the conviction in my voice, that these four words express what I feel. They can look behind them and discover the depth and width and height of my passion for language. You, too, can sound convincing about the subject you feel passionate about.

If you think the word *passion* is too strong, ease up on it a little, but still keep the conviction in your voice.

DRONING ON

So many times we meet people who drone on about their hobbies, their beliefs, their loves, and their hates, yet their voices don't even express passion with the small *p*. There is little to let you sense their real feelings.

Then we come across people who raise the tempo and the temperature. We can tell what their subjects mean to them. They don't have to shout about it—some of the most passionate speakers are soft-spoken—but the essence of their feeling is there, and that's what counts.

A WAY WITH WORDS

The PASSIONATE speakers have a way with words, use word pictures, and, because they are confident within themselves, are not afraid to reveal their thoughts and dreams and emotions.

Some people are so terrified at the very thought of expressing themselves with any kind of passion that they creep inside themselves and do just the opposite. They are not doing themselves justice. A little passion is better than none at all.

You may not express **PASSION!** in your speech immediately, if ever, but you can certainly climb up from that mild little passion and create for yourself an image of a more dynamic and convincing communicator.

It's all very well

being

PROFESSIONALS

but

we also need to

like

professionals

A SOUND LIKE NO OTHER

Over the years, the number of professionals I've met who sounded *unprofessional* makes me wonder if they ever listened to their own voices.

Probably not. Long periods of study and theory and practice in chosen careers can deaden anyone's sense of sound.

But start climbing, begin to assert authority, have to give talks, represent a company, or be a keynote speaker, and the lack of professionalism in speech shows up.

NEVER TOO LATE

I say over and over again, "It's never too late." I've had people of all ages improve dramatically. Occasionally I meet someone who is tone deaf and can't hear the differences in sound; but most people, especially when they hear themselves on audiocassette or see and hear themselves on video, realize their lack of verbal skills.

The majority do change. Even a small improvement can alter the way they feel about themselves and sound to others. It's a real thrill when I hear people begin to express themselves with vitality and color, use descriptive words and imagery, and make language work for them instead of letting it confuse and deflate them.

THE STEPPING STONE

There's a quality about professional speech that sounds like no other. From the moment seasoned professionals open their mouths, they're different. You listen to them; you certainly can't ignore them. You may not agree with everything they say, but you take what they're talking about seriously.

Even if you're secure in your career and hold a responsible job, don't let that dissuade you from opening your ears to how you sound to others.

If you haven't got a career, keep in mind that a professional sound is a stepping stone to success.

POINT TO PONDER

how can we
become
more
CONFIDENT?

FROM FAITH TO FREEDOM

When I was a child, my parents made me believe that I could do anything. That belief has sustained me through the years. It gave me faith in myself and made me feel that by just being myself there was nothing I couldn't tackle. If you weren't inspired like this when you were young, you can absorb the philosophy now.

It's a state of mind, a feeling of confidence that overcomes many of the difficulties and upsets we all go through. If you keep telling yourself that you can do anything, little by little you *will* feel able to do anything. It will have an enormous impact on your self-esteem.

WHAT'S FAILURE?

I was also brought up to take no notice of the word *failure*. It meant little to my parents. Failures, yes, we all have them. We need them. Life would be meaningless without them. But a failure is not a disaster. Rather, it is a new beginning. And we can learn from our experience of failure.

I couldn't count the number of failures I've had, but always that sense of a new beginning has spurred me on. I laugh, and start again.

THE RISING SUN

The tarot card featuring "death" has, in the background, the rising sun.

Your failure may be something as simple as messing up a short talk in front of your peers or as important as falling apart as you give a major speech. So, think about that rising sun. Say to yourself, "So what! I'm not going to let it get me down. I'll do better next time."

But make sure you do!

Plan, prepare, practice, perform.

Have faith in yourself, even if it takes time to get to the standard you want. Once that faith is established, the freedom that comes with it will help you to avoid failures in the future.

Why do people sound

from one another?

IT'S ALL ABOUT COLOR

I've got a thing about color. I believe that each of us speaks with our own special blend of color.

Here's a breakdown of what voice color conveys to me.

White, beige, gray—these are the flat, dreary, boring voices, the ones that make you tune out as soon as they start talking.

Yellow—a young voice, still immature. Some people carry this color throughout their lives and never really sound grown-up.

Pink—a warmer version of yellow, with plenty of personality, but still young.

Brown—very much a country voice. A little rough about the edges but sincere and easy on the ear.

Green—a really natural voice, whether educated or not. Good to listen to because there is no affectation.

Blue—cold! Have you ever listened to someone with a blue voice? No emotion, nothing to make you feel welcome. A voice that talks *at* you not *to* you.

Red—a delightful voice filled with vibrancy and lots of life.

Purple—over the top! I once had lunch with an actor who told the most *marvelous* stories and never let anyone get a word in—a true purple.

Silver—a clear, bell-like voice, not overly emotional, but lovely to listen to.

Gold—Every now and again nature creates a golden voice that is so enchanting, that once it is heard, it's never forgotten. A man can have a golden voice just as easily as a woman.

All of us vary according to our moods. We may be gray when we're tired or grumpy but switch to red when something exciting happens.

But most of us have an overriding color—one that people know us by. If this happens to be blue or white, we should brighten it up. A purple voice may need to be toned down just a little.

If you don't know what color your voice is, ask a trusted friend. Otherwise listen intently to yourself, perhaps on tape.

The third category is

TECHNIQUE

IF

our lips never move, we'll be talking to ourselves

we speak behind clenched teeth, our voice won't carry

we have a lazy tongue, we could get tongue-tied

our breathing is shallow, we have to gasp for air

our resonance is poor, our voice will sound thin

our vowels are flat, our speech will be harsh

our speech is sloppy, our enunciation is poor

we don't open our mouths, we won't be heard

If you think none of this matters

YOU'RE FOOLING YOURSELF

SPRUCE UP!

So, it pays to take time to spruce up your technique with exercises that will help you to speak so that people can hear you, *admire your voice,* and *enjoy talking to you.* Actually, all of the exercises are very simple. But like many simple things in life, we don't bother to do them until we realize just how important they are.

START EARLY!

In many cases, a *child* would have no trouble doing the exercises the first time. In fact, people often ask me, "Why didn't I learn these when I was a child?" Why didn't you? I did, and I've never regretted it.

When we start early, the results of the exercises soon become part of our pattern of speech and this lays the foundation for good speech later on.

It's important to remember though that no matter when you start or what age you are, if you *persevere* the results will be good. I've seen people in their sixties begin to improve their voices and they have as much success as young people.

SECRET OF SUCCESS

If I told you to practice every day for twenty minutes, you'd probably do just that, for a few days. Then it would be ten minutes, later down to five, and before long you'd have given up altogether.

The secret of doing exercises consistently is to inject them into your *normal routine,* something you do every day anyway.

For instance, it's great doing them in the bath or the shower (no one can see or hear you). If you have a car, practice while you're driving. Many people do this. I often hear funny stories of those who have been diligently pushing out their lips or twisting their tongues being given strange looks by drivers in other cars! Who cares? The important thing is that you are really helping yourself. It's regularity that counts. Little and often. Little and often.

Here are some simple exercises to get you started.

LIP EXERCISES

THE KISS AND THE GRIN

Push your lips forward as far as they will go. Not in a tight, tense way, but easily, as though you were going to *kiss* somebody. Then bring them back as far as they will go—like a big *grin*—without showing your teeth. Repeat six times. You'll find the muscles around your mouth react quickly.

WHISTLE

By thrusting your lips forward, you're actually stretching them. *Whistling* is a good exercise because no one knows that you're doing an exercise! You can whistle any old tune, anytime.

SPEAK WITH YOUR TEETH SHUT

For this, all you have to do is *close your teeth* but keep the lips open. Speak in an exaggerated manner, about anything at all, so that your lips move in a rather unnatural way. *But they must move.* If you mutter away with them almost shut, you're defeating the purpose of the exercise.

SPEAK WITH A CORK (PENCIL, FINGERTIP) IN THE MOUTH

This exercise is to push the teeth a little apart so that the *lips* have to work even harder. Talk about the weather, your favorite TV program, or even say a nursery rhyme. The main thing is that you talk. It's an easy way to strengthen the lip muscles.

MOUTHING THE WORDS

Our lips play an important part in our speech. If they don't move properly, it makes it difficult for us to form words correctly.

Take a good look at someone (the television is ideal for this). When he speaks, what does he do with his lips?

Does the person's top lip move at all? We call this the "stiff upper lip." It makes for a rigid form of speech.

Does neither lip move? If so, the person is mumbling behind a barrier and it will be difficult for you, or anyone else, to hear what he's saying.

Is there partial movement of both lips? This helps, but it's still a long way from perfect.

Is there really good lip movement? This is interesting to watch because every sound is given the right vehicle to create words. The lips should move a lot and constantly change shape.

ORGANS OF SPEECH

The lips are among our *articulative organs*, the organs with which we produce speech. The others are the tongue, teeth, upper and lower jaw, and the hard and soft palates.

Because they're made up of muscle, the lips can become tired and a bit lazy. To combat this, a few exercises on a regular basis do wonders for keeping the lips in good condition.

A MOLD

A face with a mouth that is set in a firm mold never looks professional. All you get is speech that is difficult, and sometimes impossible, to hear and sounds that are often flat or harsh.

It's interesting to observe people who speak different languages. Their lip movements vary considerably. A tip for learning another language is to study the lip movements of those who speak it well.

TONGUE EXERCISES

CURLING THE TONGUE

Put your lips into the position needed to say the vowel *oo* (as in *room*). Put your tongue out. Bring your lips around your tongue so that the tongue is forced upwards at the sides. Slowly bring your tongue in so that it curls as it goes. Slide your tongue in and out, maintaining that curl all the time. Repeat six times.

BRING TONGUE IN SLOWLY

Put your tongue out as far as it will go, then *very slowly* bring it in. You'll feel the tension underneath the tongue. This helps to strengthen the muscles. Repeat six times.

MOVE TONGUE SLOWLY FROM SIDE TO SIDE

Put your tongue out and to one side. Move it *very slowly* to the other side without touching the teeth. Repeat six times.

POINT AND BROADEN THE TONGUE

Put your tongue out and point it at the tip, then broaden it so that the tongue flattens from side to side. Don't let it touch the teeth. Repeat six times. This is a more advanced exercise, so don't worry if you can't do it right away.

POKE THE TONGUE

Put your hand over one cheek. Press the tip of the tongue into the cheek. Hold for six seconds. Do the same with the other cheek. This is based on an isometric exercise, where you strengthen muscles by *contracting* rather than *stretching* them. Repeat six times.

THE TIRELESS TONGUE

Of all the organs of speech, the tongue works the hardest. It's constantly on the go, tripping here and skipping there. No wonder it has to be in top condition to keep up with the demand on its services.

If you don't believe me, just say a poem or a nursery rhyme very slowly. Let the words roll around in your mouth. You'll discover that even within one word, the tongue may have to *change position* three or four times, or more.

Like the lips, the tongue is made up mainly of *muscle*. That's why it must be kept in good working order. A lazy tongue is a disaster. We slur our words and people keep asking us to repeat ourselves.

COULDN'T SPEAK

But never get carried away and do too many exercises too quickly! I once had a student who had a lazy tongue. So anxious was she to get her tongue flexible that she overdid the exercises. The next time I saw her she had a big swollen tongue and she mumbled to me, "Maarriiee, III ccaann'tt ssppeeaakk!"

The tongue is like any other muscle in our body. We'd never think of playing golf or tennis for a whole afternoon if we hadn't played for a year or so. If we did, we'd suffer the same agony.

SUPER TONGUE

But practice we should—little and often, and away from other people's aston- ished gaze. As our tongue gets stronger, it's able to cope with all the strains and stresses of everyday talking.

When it becomes a super tongue, it'll make us feel much more confident about mounting a platform and speaking clearly and distinctly in public.

Until we notice our tongue and realize how important it is to us, we never appreciate it properly. Yet our tongue is at the heart of everything we say.

Imagine life without it!

JAW EXERCISES

MOVING THE JAW

Move the lower jaw from side to side. Do it very slowly so as not to make it feel as though you've dislocated it!

THE YAWN

Yawning is a marvelous way of making the jaws work. They really have to move and it gives you the feeling of what efficient jaws should be like. The only problem is that once you start yawning, you keep on doing it.

INFLECTION

CHANGING THE PITCH

I want you to think of your voice as a piano! Starting on as low a note as possible, go up the scale saying the word, *rise*. When you reach the highest note you feel comfortable with, start coming down, saying the word, *fall*. Again go as low as you feel you can manage without straining your voice. This is an excellent way to discover your range of pitch.

ENUNCIATION

Say these words very slowly. Discover how the organs of speech come together to produce the sounds and how hard the tongue has to work.

Softest silk	Cold showers	Black coats	Blowing bubbles
New clothes	Masked balls	Flaked snow	Milk crates

A NEW WAY OF SPEAKING

These exercises may appear to be very simple, but don't underestimate them. They give you that extra edge, with increased nerve and muscle control, that is needed to produce clear, crisp, accurate speech. The trouble with so many people is that they don't have this edge. The result? Sloppy speech, inarticulate language, and the embarrassment of having to repeat themselves again and again, because others simply can't understand what they're talking about.

OPENING THE MOUTH

Let's look at the jaws. We don't think about them much at all. The only time I'm really aware of how they're constructed is when I see a skeleton. Yet unless they're working properly everything we say gets locked in behind them. I've seen people who move their lips well, but don't open their jaws and of course their speech is not good. Make them move! Yawn and yawn and yawn, even if you feel like yawning for ages afterwards. It's a great way of making those jaws open.

Moving the lower jaw from side to side is helpful too. It helps to loosen the jaw up so that it's more mobile.

THE RANGE

The exercise for changing pitch is excellent. I can usually tell exactly what a person's vocal range is after hearing them do it. It shows up the areas where the pitch is weak, or nonexistent. If you're aware, for instance, that you have a fairly light voice, concentrate on the lower notes, pushing your boundary a little further each time. This helps to develop a deeper voice. A voice that has little light and shade needs to concentrate on rising a little higher each time.

Many words may sound simple to say, but sometimes they are not. They present us with quite a difficult combination of tongue, teeth, lips, and so on. That's why I suggested saying the groups of words on the previous page very slowly. By rolling them around in your mouth you get a better understanding of how hard the tongue has to work, and how it combines with the other organs of speech.

BREATHING EXERCISES

COUNTING ON ONE BREATH

Take a deep breath through the nose, then start counting—one, two, three... Go as far as is comfortable, speaking *clearly and distinctly.* Don't slur your words. A woman should get to around 50. A man—with a larger lung capacity—should make 100 or more. This simple exercise gives you a good idea of how efficient your breathing is. Each time you do the exercise you'll find that your count will go higher.

FIVE TIMES FIVE

Take a deep breath through the nose, count to five *out loud,* then count to five *mentally,* another five out loud, another five mentally until your breath gives out. This strengthens your breathing technique and ensures that while you're counting mentally your air isn't escaping through your nose because your rib cage keeps falling.

WORDS ON ONE BREATH

Repeat each of the following sentences as many times as you can on one breath.

1. It's never too late to learn.
2. Deep breathing calms my nerves and makes my voice sound better.
3. I know I can go out and capture an audience, make them sit up and listen to me, so that they'll remember everything I've said.

Repeat each of the following sentences as many times as you can on one breath putting the emphasis on the words that are underlined.

1. The exercises are simple, *but I must do them every day!*
2. If we win the debate *what a celebration we'll have!*
3. I can communicate with confidence and style, *but I've got to use the six Ps!*

THE BREATH OF LIFE

If we don't breathe, we don't live, let alone speak! But there is breathing and *breathing*. The lungs themselves are made up of tissue and can't be controlled. The only thing we have control over is giving them a *space* in which to expand.

Basically we can breathe in three ways.

We can raise our shoulders so that the rib cage goes up and down, but the lungs are not given this space to expand. This leads to shallow breathing. While we're asleep we breathe with the tummy going in and out, as we do during yoga exercises, but that too prevents the lungs from having space.

Shallow breathing results in us not having enough air left to finish a sentence so that we have to take a gulp of air in the middle. This sounds amateurish. A speaker with good breathing can flow on from one sentence to another effortlessly.

THE BELLOWS

In speech, we use what's called the intercostal-diaphragmatic method of breathing. The intercostal muscles hold the ribs together, while the diaphragm (a powerful muscle at the base of the lungs) is like a bellows to pump air.

Try this. Stand up and put your hands at the base of your ribs, with fingertips touching in the center of your body. Breathe out, then breathe in deeply. You'll find that the rib cage, plus the floating ribs at the base, will come out and your diaphragm will expand upwards and outwards.

Now the lungs have a whole cavity to fill and they'll do just that by puffing up with air. Breathing like this gives your speech strength.

CONTROLLING THE MUSCLES

The main problem with breathing is poor muscle control, just as in the lips and tongue. When the intercostal muscles and the diaphragm are weak, our speech suffers because they can't perform properly. But by doing simple exercises on a regular basis we can strengthen them.

POINT TO PONDER

how can we
sound
more
RESONANT?

THE SIMPLE HUM

Poor resonance really can wreck a person's appeal. She sounds *nasal,* can't be heard properly, and has a *harsh quality* to her voice. Who needs that?

Resonance is the added vibrations given to the tones of the voice. Speech sounds are amplified by sympathetic vibrations in the bone structure of the head and chest and by directing the air column well forward into the resonating cavities of the mouth, nose, and pharynx (the cavity behind the mouth and the nose). A problem arises when the air column *doesn't quite hit its target.*

THE VIOLIN

If we speak badly, the chances are that the muscles around the throat are tight and the air column has lost its way. The result is a voice that has *little carrying power.* I once saw a man speaking on a street corner. I was quite close to him, but although he was putting an enormous amount of effort and emotion into his speech, I could hardly hear a word.

Think of it another way. You're playing a violin. Someone puts a hand on your instrument, what happens? Yes, the sound goes dead. The vibrations stop, so there's *no resonance.*

Some people speak with an irritating "twang." The air column is not coming forward enough into the mouth. It's ending up mainly in the nasal cavity.

HUMMING

A rich, resonant voice is one that does hit its target. It fills all the cavities and comes well forward into the mouth.

The best exercise I know to get a resonant voice is humming. You hum until *your lips tingle.* They tingle because the air is vibrating through the lips. If you're doing it well, the tingling becomes so intense that you feel like scratching your lips away.

Hum. If there's no tingling, start again. Hum, say *ma-ma-ma-ma-ma.* Hum. Repeat and repeat until there is.

CONSONANTS

The nuts and bolts of speech

Sounds

that are

stopped

—or partially stopped—

by one of the

ORGANS OF SPEECH

THE SKELETON

Consonants can be thought of as the skeleton of our language. They provide the framework on which we build our words. They should be polished, sharp, and clear.

There are 24 consonants. These are divided into nine *aspirate* (or breathy sounds, where the air passes through the vocal cords unvocalized) and 15 *vocal* consonants (where all the air is turned into sound).

Here is a list of the sounds.

ASPIRATE			VOCAL		
P	as in	pipe	B	as in	bed
T	as in	tent	D	as in	dog
K	as in	kick	G	as in	gun
S	as in	seat	Z	as in	zeal
F	as in	fire	V	as in	veal
H	as in	he	Y	as in	you
WH	as in	wheel	W	as in	woe
TH	as in	thin	TH	as in	them
SH	as in	shoe	NG	as in	sing
			L	as in	love
			M	as in	mail
			N	as in	nail
			R	as in	road
			R	as in	war
			Z	as in	azure

Say each of these words carefully, discovering just what the consonants sound like. You'll see that a number are *similiar*—P and B for example—yet one has a distinctly breathy sound whereas the other has not. Say each sound as it starts off the word rather than as you would say it in the alphabet.

It's equally important to say the sounds distinctly when they're in the *middle* or at the *end* of words. The consonants give a voice the clarity of speech we all strive for. As you practice, you'll find *how* the sounds are stopped by combinations of the tongue, lips, teeth, upper and lower jaws, hard and soft palates.

Vowels

Vowels

VOWELS

Vowels

The music of our language

How

A – E – I – O – U

can change our life

MAGICAL MUSIC

Vowels are the powerhouse of speech and the music of our language. Consonants by themselves are static sounds. Vowels add the magic.

We tell the difference between people who sound superb when they speak and those whose voices are harsh and unpleasant to the ear by the way they say their vowels.

Vowels are *pure* sounds, made in the larynx or voice box. From there they flow through the mouth with nothing to stop them—no lips or tongue to get in the way. Rather they depend on the way the lips and tongue are *shaped* to give the exact sound of the vowel we want to say.

We always think of the five vowels. Actually there are 18 vowels, because each one has a variety of sounds. There are five *As,* three *Es,* two *Is,* five *Os,* and three *Us:*

A	as in	name, make, fame	AH	as in	bath, laugh, father
ă	as in	lack, man, shall	AW	as in	cause, stalk, northern
air	as in	chair, stare, fair			
EE	as in	speak, seek, meal	ĕ	as in	yes, seven, second
er	as in	learn, herd, worship			
I	as in	like, shine, ice	ĭ	as in	it, live, mission
OH	as in	home, roam, clothes	OW	as in	shout, mouth, owl
OI	as in	voice, point, boy	ŏ	as in	dog, jog, stop
OO	as in	too, who, school			
U	as in	new, few, tune	u	as in	full, bull, butcher
ŭ	as in	up, flutter, fun			

Because each accent or dialect is different, the way we say our vowels varies, but this list is a guide to how many basic vowel sounds there are.

To thoroughly learn this technical side of speech you should go to a qualified speech or linguistics teacher.

I want you to do something for me

Here is a word

Moon

(as in the sky)

Think about it

Write down as many
words you associate
with the moon
as you can

Take about a minute

BEGIN NOW!

LESSON IN LOGIC

If you're like most people, you've included in your list words like *yellow, stars, blue, cheese, crescent, man-in-the-moon, tides, sky, moonlight, rocket, moon river, craters, astronaut, eclipse, lady of the night, rotation, moonbeam, bright, weightlessness,* and so on. That's fine. Except a list like this is all *jumbled up.* It jumps from one image to another. There's no *pattern* to it.

If you were trying to convey information about the moon to someone what chance would they have of making any sense of it? Very little, I expect.

THE CHART

Now I'd like you to look at the next page and see how I've recorded my words about the moon. I've drawn a chart with a circle in the middle. On the outside of the circle, the chart is like a clock, so it's important that we have a line at 12 o'clock, a quarter past, half past, and a quarter to, plus as many other divisions as we may need. I devised this method of recording material years ago, and am still getting amazing feedback from it. It's like a memory map, but simpler.

You'll see that I've put the word *moon* in the *middle.*

Then in the space following the 12 o'clock line (we always start there) I've entered the words I feel are the first I need to describe the moon itself: ridges, craters, moon dust, moon rock, moonscape. Then, in a logical manner, I've gone clockwise and built up my picture, section by section, so that a listener could follow my reasoning. In every case—and this is important—I've put a title or heading at the top of the divisions and <u>underlined</u> it. I call these sections *categories.*

A CLEAR WORD PICTURE

Look at the chart again. If I placed the words haphazardly from different categories, I'd end up with a list as jumbled as before. By giving each category its rightful place in my chart I can present a clear picture by simply glancing at the chart. Try making your own chart and entering your list of words, under their category headings, and see how much clearer your word picture is.

THE MOON

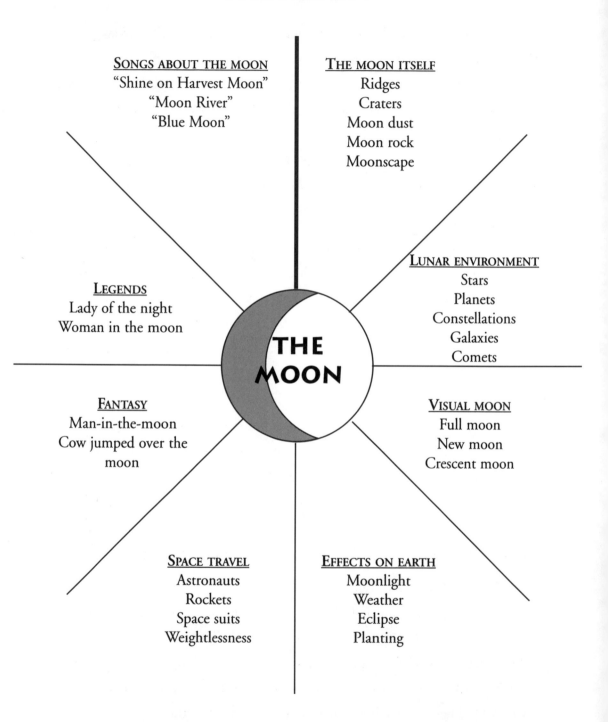

SONGS ABOUT THE MOON
"Shine on Harvest Moon"
"Moon River"
"Blue Moon"

THE MOON ITSELF
Ridges
Craters
Moon dust
Moon rock
Moonscape

LEGENDS
Lady of the night
Woman in the moon

LUNAR ENVIRONMENT
Stars
Planets
Constellations
Galaxies
Comets

THE MOON

FANTASY
Man-in-the-moon
Cow jumped over the moon

VISUAL MOON
Full moon
New moon
Crescent moon

SPACE TRAVEL
Astronauts
Rockets
Space suits
Weightlessness

EFFECTS ON EARTH
Moonlight
Weather
Eclipse
Planting

SIMPLICITY ITSELF

What you now do is use the same "moon chart" when you have to give a *speech* or even a short talk. Where I put the word *moon* in the first chart, you now record the title of your talk. By thinking out the overall plan of your speech, you break it up into categories, underline the headings, and add as many key words as you wish in each section. The beauty of this is that when you give your speech, you only have one piece of paper. A glance now and then is all you need.

I've frequently seen people sit in front of my video camera and try to talk on a subject they know well. They fail because they get muddled in their thinking and there's no logic to what they say. Their talk peters out after a minute or two.

THEY'RE OFF!

Then I show them the moon chart and instruct them how to use it. Having studied it, they can immediately speak on the same subject confidently and rationally for ten minutes or more. It's exciting to watch.

Another plus is the fact that you can prepare material on a variety of subjects—for meetings, conferences, or whatever—and file them away to be used at any time. It saves a lot of work not having to think out the subject again and again. People use it for essays, documents, working out plots for stories and books. I like it because it's so easy to use. If you're speaking, you don't have to rustle through lots of papers or cards. If you know your subject, you only need the key words.

NO NOTES

Because I don't use notes or a script when I speak, it may seem as though everything is totally spontaneous. But the best speeches are not. They're carefully planned.

So I do my planning on a moon chart before I go. Sometimes I use several; crossing out, changing categories and key words around, working out which is the most logical order to use. When I'm happy, I photograph the final moon chart in my mind, and then leave it behind. The chart helps me manage time too—I always know where I should be at a given time: halfway through or coming to a conclusion.

YOUR MOON CHART

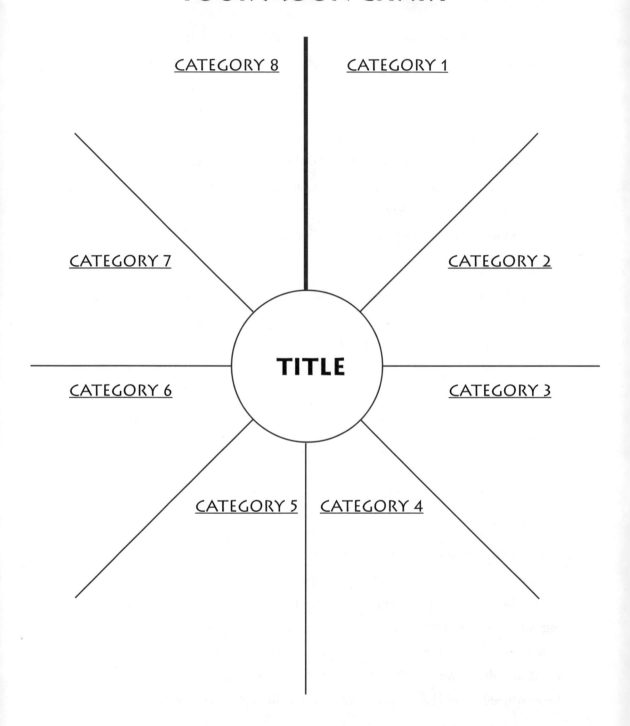

CATEGORY 8

CATEGORY 1

CATEGORY 7

CATEGORY 2

TITLE

CATEGORY 6

CATEGORY 3

CATEGORY 5

CATEGORY 4

WHAT TO DO WITH IT

Now that you've got your own moon chart, start using it. Practice with a variety of subjects. Start with simple ones. Get your categories first, underline them, then fill in the key words underneath.

The word I always start people off with is *road*. Sounds easy, doesn't it? Yet by the time they have finished with it, most of them are amazed at the long list of both categories and key words they have compiled, from what a road is made from, to people who use it, to the abstract.

ROAD

<u>Construction</u>—concrete, asphalt, gravel, paved, dirt, cobblestone...

<u>Names</u>—street, avenue, boulevard, drive, lane, terrace, circle, place, court...

<u>Markings</u>—parking lines, yellow lines, double lines, crossings, arrows...

<u>Signs</u>—stop, caution, children crossing, railroad crossing, school...

<u>Vehicles</u>—cars, vans, trailers, trucks, buses, caravans, motorcycles...

<u>People</u>—business people, tourists, joggers, hikers, police, bikers...

<u>Functions</u>—transport, communication, physical fitness, freight...

<u>Animals</u>—dogs, cats, horses, cattle, sheep, raccoons, rabbits, frogs...

<u>Scenery</u>—gardens, houses, churches, shops, fields, farms, rivers...

<u>Plants</u>—trees, hedges, grass, weeds, flowers, wild flowers, shrubs...

<u>Roadworks</u>—shovels, bulldozers, concrete mixers, water trucks, flags...

<u>Accessories</u>—footpaths, drains, underground cables, curbs, poles...

<u>Rules</u>—traffic law, speed limits, age limits, blood alcohol limit, vehicles...

<u>Accidents</u>—crashes, collisions, speed, alcohol, pedestrians, fatigue...

<u>Road breaks</u>—railroads, bridges, intersections, cattle crossings, barriers...

<u>Songs</u>—"Road to Morocco," "Rocky Road," "Yellowbrick Road"....

<u>Abstract</u>—Road to Knowledge, Road to Freedom, Road to Success...

WORDS WHEN YOU WANT THEM

It's not only fun compiling lists like this, it's also very good for your ability to think of a host of words when you want them.

Now let's think about

MAKING A SPEECH

YOUR ONE CHANCE

When you're standing in front of an audience, you can't run away and hide. Somehow or other you've got to get through that speech. If it doesn't go well, the danger lies in the next time you have to give a speech. Will you make another blunder? Make a fool of yourself? Make your audience embarrassed by your lack of professionalism? It's like a vicious cycle that feeds on lack of confidence: it puts fear into you, makes you tremble at the very thought of standing up in public and doing what should come naturally. But you can *break* that cycle.

HITTING YOUR TARGET

If this is your problem, keep in mind that if your audience has difficulty understanding an article in a newspaper, they can read it again and again until they do.

With speech, they cannot do this. You've got to *hit your target the first time*. Until you're more confident, go step by step, so that you feel you have a really good chance of coming across well.

Step 1: *Plan your speech*, even if it's just to be delivered in front of a few colleagues. Use the moon chart. With this, you know you've covered all the relevant material and have a strong opening and closing.

PULL OUT THE STOPS

Step 2: *Write your speech* based on your moon chart and read it *out loud* until it has an easy-to-say flow. Get rid of clichés, difficult or old-fashioned words, and phraseology. Throw out jargon and alliteration. *Keep it simple.*

Step 3: *Vitalize your speech*. Put the *color* in! Give words and phrases their full value so that your audience has to listen.

Step 4: *Talk your speech*. Make sure you *open your mouth* and say your words clearly and distinctly.

Step 5: *Have confidence in your speech*. Stand up and *do it!*

If you can manage all these things, you're almost certain to get your message across in fine style. And next time it's sure to be easier.

Because of the difference between

WRITTEN

and

SPOKEN LANGUAGE

it's imperative you read every sentence

ALOUD

again and again, and even again,

until you get the

flow

of the

SPOKEN WORD

READING THE WRITTEN WORD ALOUD

Many people, particularly those in business, plan their speech, write their speech, and only then do they try to say it!

What comes out is not fluent, flowing speech at all. It's a garbled mass of written-style words and phraseology. It's stilted. It's stultifying. It's sluggish. What looks good to the *eye* can offend the *ear*.

CHANGING LANGUAGE

Language is constantly evolving. Listen to a recording of someone speaking say, 50 years ago, and you'll hear pompous, dated language. We don't speak like that anymore. We use a freer style, even in public.

Although written language has changed, too, it has changed less than the spoken word. The difference between the two is definitely there.

We *write,* "I am," "he is," "we are not," "I will not," and so on.

But we *say,* "I'm," "he's," "we aren't," "I won't"—unless we want to be very specific and use words like, "I cannot," "I will not."

We *write* more formally and grammatically in a structured sense.

We *speak* easily with little formality, sometimes ungrammatically, colloquially, often using the vernacular.

We may *write* complicated sentences that the eye can translate effortlessly.

We never *speak* like that, otherwise we get caught up in tangles.

AGAIN AND AGAIN

That's why the best advice is to read your speech, sentence by sentence aloud, over and over again. Listen, analyze, and change if necessary. You may have to switch sentences around, throw out tricky alliteration that could prove too hard to say, chase away the heavily structured, the prissy, the dated.

In this book I've deliberately used a style that combines the written and the spoken word because I want you to read the pages out loud.

How does speech relate to

fashion?

À LA MODE

Fashion affects many aspects of our lives, and speech is no exception. Language too follows patterns we have to be aware of if we wish to remain contemporary in our approach. It isn't difficult to pick out those who have been left behind in the constantly changing linguistic fashions. They use out-of-date phraseology, old-fashioned constructions, and dated words. It's as though they're from another world.

These are the exceptions, of course. But even if we're only a *few years behind the norm* we can place ourselves in a different time frame. It's all a matter of keeping in touch. Keeping in touch with quality language. Keeping in touch with how that language is being spoken.

OVER THE TOP

The language we use reflects our age too. When older people listen to the young discussing their music or their morals it's like tuning into outer space. We don't understand half of what they say because they have their own vocabulary and own way of using it, and a lot of their words have hidden meanings. In time this might change. They may have to adapt to the norm to be able to find work, study, or play a part in their community. Youth always has had a different way of speaking and communicating, so this is nothing new.

My advice to worried parents is always, "Don't hassle them or you'll make the situation worse!" It's surprising how even the most inarticulate teenagers can adapt to a better way of speaking when they're ready—if they've got role models to learn from.

Of course they can always be encouraged to join a drama club or a singing group, or take lessons in speech and communication.

BE AWARE

Generally speaking, we all have to be aware of the new words and phraseology that are creeping into our language. There has been a rush of these in recent years with the computer age and high-tech, global communication changing every day. It's a constant learning process.

A speech is more
than a means of getting information across

It has to
CAPTURE THE IMAGINATION
REINFORCE ITS MESSAGE
CONSTANTLY KEEP THE AUDIENCE
on its toes

And it does this with a skillful blend of
VOICE
FACIAL EXPRESSION
GESTURE
and
BODY LANGUAGE

THE BLEND

The face can *mirror* a voice. If that sounds like a sweeping statement, think of talking to someone on the telephone. Can you tell when he's smiling, just by the sound of his voice?

If you were looking at a speaker on television and had the sound turned down, you would still have a fairly good idea of her ability to speak well. A dull speaker usually has a dull face with little expression, no life in the eyes, and a somewhat downcast appearance and body language.

THE TRICKS

A speaker with a *lively face and bright eyes* captures you because of her vitality. The voice usually bubbles along filled with color and impressive word pictures. The body language and specific gestures fit in naturally with what is being said. And the speaker employs every trick in the book (this book!) to hold the attention of the audience. You can't become a quality speaker by simply waving a magic wand, but it's amazing how you can use that wand to help you along the way. It takes time. It's impossible to pick out one attribute and say, "If you do this or that, you'll be a successful speaker."

SPEAK OUT

First, you have to build up your confidence. Start small and quietly inject professionalism into your speech.

Don't be afraid to *speak out*. Surprisingly enough this seems to give people more trouble than anything else. But speaking out reinforces your confidence; not speaking out drains it.

Then add a touch of magic to your speech: Use your word pictures. Put your heart into what you're saying. Never repeat, parrot-fashion, what someone else has said or what you've written down.

Leave your audience with a clear message that they'll remember.

Can we learn
BODY LANGUAGE?

DOING WHAT COMES NATURALLY

Body language has become something of a cult subject since it was "discovered" not so long ago. Now there are many studies, books, and videos devoted to it. I, too, have written a book on body language, for children, but I can't help thinking that too much has been made of it all.

Of course it's possible to study the language of the body and to learn—and you should do just that—but like any personal habit, a contrived reaction looks like what it is, contrived, and therefore unnatural.

The basis of good body language is *confidence*. If we haven't got confidence, then we're merely dabbling with it. If body language is to work in a positive way, then its underlying elements have to be tackled.

THE BASICS

If you're worried about your body language, start with the basics. Get rid of any nervous habits: turning your rings, licking your lips, wringing your hands, flicking imaginary fluff from your clothes, fiddling with a pen or your hair, continually looking at your watch (unless there's a reason), constant movement of your legs, tapping a foot, and scratching—anywhere! If you aren't aware of what you do, ask a friend. It is possible to control habits like these through strict mental discipline. I've often been amused to see people who have "learned" body language. They do everything right: they sit with their body forward, legs crossed towards you, looking eager and smiling, yet sometimes I get the impression that it's all window dressing. That makes me wary.

THE SECRET

A really confident person is relaxed, with easy movements when sitting, standing, or walking. You can sense it immediately. The secret is to *be yourself.* Put all your efforts into becoming a relaxed and confident person. Take the trouble to learn how to speak well and how to interact with others. Then natural body language will follow.

The day has come!

You're off to face an

AUDIENCE

TIPS FOR SUCCESS

Whether you're going to give a talk at your local club, a speech at a conference, an interview on radio, or appear on television what can you do to *prepare* yourself?

Well, obviously, you have to do your *homework*. You must be familiar with the background of your topic, know the facts and figures, and have confidence in your material, whether it is written down or still in your head.

Try to get a good night's sleep before the day you are to speak. When you're under any sort of pressure or stress you need to be in as good a *physical* state as possible.

WELL GROOMED

It should go without saying, but being *well groomed* from tip to toe is important. Polished shoes, pressed pants, run-free panty hose, dandruff-free jackets, unchipped nail polish, good makeup, shining hair, clean teeth, clean hands, clean body. Sometimes I'm shocked to see how little attention is given to these things by those who should know better.

Look at yourself in a mirror before you leave home. When you're sure you're well groomed forget about your appearance.

If your lips are dry don't lick them. If you do, they'll get drier still. Put a light coat of petroleum jelly over them. When they're well lubricated, you won't have the urge to lick. Licking the lips always makes people look nervous.

If your hands feel sticky, run cold water over them. Don't forget the antiperspirant for the armpits. You don't want to show signs of perspiring.

A CUP OF TEA

Keep off the booze! The effects could be disastrous, and you could end up with a red nose. Instead, before you leave home, have a cup of tea with two large teaspoonfuls of sugar in it. This gives you instant energy and calms the nerves. Move your neck and shoulders around gently to relieve tension and take several deep breaths. Deep breathing helps the voice as well as makes you feel calmer. And *hum. Hum. Hum.* Until your lips *tingle, tingle, tingle.*

Some people feel you should always

start a speech with a

JOKE (!)

but unless you're very good at telling jokes

PLEASE DON'T

A badly told, corny, or tasteless joke is an

EMBARRASSMENT

BEWARE OF THE JOKE

There's nothing that puts you at a disadvantage more quickly than having mucked up a joke, or worse, forgotten the punch line.

If this happens you could well continue your speech in a cloud of humiliation.

LISTEN AND LEARN

Listen carefully to other speakers.

How do *they* tell jokes? Are they successful? Do people laugh? Or do they snicker as though embarrassed?

Listen to the *type* of jokes told. Are they risqué? Or downright rude? Perhaps heavy-handed? Do you lose interest quickly?

Listen to the *way* they tell them. Have they the kind of voices that deliver a witty turn of a phrase? Do they plod along? Are they under pressure while telling them?

Listen to the *style* of joke told. Is it a first person experience? A hackneyed joke? A joke that has a particularly definite or catch-phrase ending?

MORTIFIED

I can never forget one conference I attended. The speaker had a fine voice, was confident to the point of being arrogant, and told one tasteless, vulgar joke after another. What upset me was that some people in the audience, obviously as vulgar as he was, laughed, shouted, and yelled their appreciation, while I, and many other sensitive souls, sat in utter mortification!

In such a case, you may win over a few with that kind of joke, but overall I do not advise it. It's always better to err on the side of good taste.

I never tell a joke when speaking, that is, one of those carefully prepared jokes. I can never remember them properly! But I do love to tell funny stories from real life. I can build up the characters and give them a special voice and put a little drama into the episode.

If you're inexperienced at telling jokes, you might be more comfortable with funny anecdotes, too. If you know you can tell a story well, go for it!

Let's say you've made a good beginning, then

OH! H-O-R-R-O-R!

your mind **goes blank**

There's so much you want to say but you

CAN'T THINK OF A SINGLE THING

WHAT DO YOU DO?

DON'T PANIC!

When your mind goes blank in front of an audience, the fear is that:

A. You'll stand like an idiot and feel foolish.

B. You'll shuffle through your papers looking for who-knows-what.

C. You'll try to continue, stammering or stuttering, and make it worse.

D. You'll be so mortified, you'll never want to speak in public again.

KEEPING YOUR COOL

This "drying up" in front of an audience means one thing: somewhere along the line there's a dysfunction. If speakers were honest, most would admit that at some time they, too, have experienced the same thing.

When your mind goes blank, usually the thought is, "I have so much I want to say, but I can't think of a single thing."

ONE THING AT A TIME

Always remember, you can't talk about ten things at the same time. You can only talk about one. That one item can be anything.

The trick is to bring your mind down to what I call TUNNEL THOUGHT and say something, even if it's only a comment about the weather.

If you're absolutely stuck for something to say, make a remark to the audience. "It's great to see so many people here tonight!"; "Am I making myself clear?"; "You're a very patient audience!"; or whatever.

OVER THE HUMP

If you can't face even that, simply say with a laugh, "I'm new to this, so please have patience with me!" People will sympathize; they've probably all gone through the same thing, but they'll get embarrassed if you just stand and stare at them. By speaking at all, the tension seems to ease and you get over the hump, and can continue your talk. Even if you get stuck two or three times in one talk, be happy that at least you are able to keep going.

Every time you introduce a

NEW THOUGHT OR IDEA

into your speech you must

STOP!

Lift your voice
and *punch* out your message

If you don't, your audience won't fully realize
you're on to something different

AND THEY MAY MISS THE POINT

EACH NEW THOUGHT

The ability to really punch out a new thought or idea can transform your speech from a rather drab recitation to one that is alive and kicking.

Think for a moment of how an inexperienced radio newscaster sounds. She reads the first news item. Then without pausing or changing the pitch of her voice, she goes straight on to the second one. What happens?

Yes, of course. She's misled you. While you were trying to figure out what sort of ending the first story had, you lost the first vital seconds of the second news item. Result? *Confusion.*

EXPERTISE

An experienced newscaster does it another way.

He reads the first item. He pauses fractionally, then with a lift of his voice he's into the second one. And you instinctively know that he's speaking about something different. Simple, isn't it?

This is how you should divide your thoughts all the time, otherwise they become confused. The ability to lift the voice and punch out your message makes all the difference. Your listeners are given the chance to take in what you're saying.

100 YEARS AGO

Look at today's newspaper. See how each item has a bold heading and several subheadings. There are also lots of new paragraphs.

When you think of newspapers 100 years ago, the type is small (like a drab voice) and the copy goes on and on, with very few paragraphs. It's difficult to concentrate on those old-fashioned papers. They're rather like a voice that drones on and on.

We need to keep our speech lively, with definite breaks for easy interpretation, then a vital new voice for each new "paragraph."

You never want to leave your audience scratching their heads wondering what you're talking about.

Gesture gesture Gesture gesture gesture Gesture gesture Gesture

HOW MUCH?

HOW OFTEN?

MAKING THE MOVES

I'm often asked, "How much gesture should you use?"

I say, "This depends *entirely on the person.*"

Why do I say that? Because gestures should never be forced or they look wooden.

You must have seen someone *try* to make a gesture—shaking a fist in the air, making an expansive gesture, wagging a finger. They gesture as though they were told what to do, and they can't quite pull it off.

PART OF THE WHOLE

A naturally expressive person may use a lot of gestures, but they're part of her personality and come naturally.

I use a lot myself, but coming from Ireland, where gesture is as natural as breathing, it's part of the way I communicate.

Other people might find such gestures impossible to do. So, if they try, what comes out is not in tune with their personalities.

The ability to use expressive gestures often goes hand in hand with confidence. A person lacking in confidence shouldn't use them because clumsy gestures look silly and convey little.

LIKE A PHONEY

However, once the confidence grows, so too does the urge to express yourself in body language as well as words. It's a great feeling.

Gesture can also have dramatic possibilities, but if it's done to excess it can have a negative effect.

The trouble with badly placed gestures is that they can make you look like a phoney, and that works against your effort to come across as a sophisticated person and a good speaker.

So my advice is

Only do what you feel happy with.

And what you feel happy with will change as time goes by.

WHAT DOES A JIGSAW PUZZLE HAVE TO DO WITH A SPEECH?

THE JIGSAW PUZZLE ILLUSION

I'll let you in on a secret. When I'm about to listen to a speech, the first thing I do is clear my mind. I make it a blank. Then into that blank I put a *jigsaw puzzle*. Why?

Because then I absorb each piece of information, its logic, its color, its appeal, its personality, if you like, and fit it into the overall picture of the puzzle.

FROM START TO FINISH

A speech that is poorly constructed or doesn't convey a clear message is like a mixed-up, discouraging jigsaw puzzle—the sort that you start and never finish.

A rambling speech tends to produce far too many pieces, maybe some from another jigsaw puzzle, so that I can't finish the one I've got in my mind.

A speech that gets off to a bad start sometimes means I put away my jigsaw puzzle before I've even begun.

But a great speech, one of superb language, brilliant word pictures, easy to follow logic, and dynamic delivery creates a jigsaw puzzle like you've never seen!

I'm quite tolerant, really, and I do try hard to make sense of what people say. However, there is a limit. There's only so much I can take before I throw my jigsaw puzzle out!

It's not my fault, as a listener, if I can't make a picture of what a speaker says. It's the speaker's fault for (1) not having prepared his speech properly; (2) not having developed his theme efficiently; and (3) not having delivered it at a reasonably professional standard.

TWO PUZZLES

I do the same thing when I judge or attend a debate, only here I have two jigsaw puzzles, one for each team.

As speaker after speaker states his or her case, the puzzle begins to fill up. The team that fills up their puzzle first, and does it better, in my mind, wins the debate and carries off the prize.

TAKING THE FATEFUL STEP

onto a platform

LOOKING DOWN

Walking onto a platform and looking out at a sea of faces when you're about to give a speech or a talk is a real challenge, whether it's at a conference, a rally, or a committee meeting. You must *prepare* yourself. Have your speech thoroughly planned, either in script form, in notes, or in your head. Be well dressed and groomed. Hum, do some deep breathing, get your shoulders back and smile to yourself.

When you take that first step, walk confidently, smile to the audience, look relaxed, acknowledge their applause. The first few seconds are *vital.* This is where you make your impression. You must succeed. I'm always reminding people of the old song, "Whenever I feel afraid...I whistle." When you whistle in a situation like this, the fear goes and so does the anxiety. *Show confidence and confidence will come,* even if you're churning up inside.

THE OPENING

How you stand is important. Space your feet a little, not too close together or too far apart. This will give you balance. If you're using a lectern, don't grip it, just put your hands on it lightly. If you're not using a lectern, you can hold your notes with one hand and either let the other hand hang loosely by your side or put it in a pocket. Personally, I dislike the old-fashioned opening, "Good evening, ladies and gentlemen. It gives me great pleasure..." I prefer a more original comment, even a rhetorical question. *Grab* your audience. Use the six Ps (page 84). Don't present your offering in a dreary, monotonous way or you'll lose them for sure.

Keep it simple and natural, yet eloquent. Be yourself—at your best. At some conferences you hear horribly *hyped-up* speeches, but who believes them?

LOOK AT THEM

Don't look down all the time, or sideways. Looking directly at your audience is especially helpful if you're feeling nervous. One interested face is all you need to get started.

TELL YOUR FRIENDS!

You're going to be **heard** on

THERE'S ONLY YOUR VOICE

This is where all the training you've done and all the exercises you've slaved over are going to come into their own. On radio, your new clothes can't be seen. On radio, the audience can't absorb your body language and expressive eyes. On radio, there's only your *voice*.

That doesn't mean you shouldn't dress well (it helps to build your confidence). It doesn't mean you shouldn't smile either. The smile puts warmth into your voice. In fact, listeners can sense a smile even if they can't see one.

THE Ps

Most important of all, try to speak *naturally*. At the same time, you must remember that only your voice is going into people's homes, so you mustn't rush it. If you do, all they'll hear is chatter.

Use *pitch, pace,* and *pause*. If you feel strongly about your cause, throw a bit of *passion* in too. Be careful about *power*, you might be overpowering for such a sensitive medium, but certainly give your talk or interview all the *professionalism* you can muster.

THE STUDIO

Before you leave home, do all the preparations for a platform performance. Arrive at the studio in good time. Running late leaves you breathless and in a state of near collapse. Radio studios are usually spartan places. You'll find a table and chairs, with a microphone and the little red cue light that lets you know when you're "on the air." There'll be a large window between the studio and the control room where the producer actually records your program or puts it on the air live.

If you're giving a talk and have a manuscript, turn up diagonal corners so that you can lift each piece of paper away easily without making a sound. If it's recorded you don't have to worry too much about messing up your lines. They can be corrected. But if you're going on live—well, that's it!

TELL EVERYBODY!

You're going to **appear** on

EYE OF THE STORM

Isn't it exciting? Isn't it terrifying? The thought of appearing in front of millions on television is one of the most frightening things for a speaker. To be so much in the public eye—in living rooms all over the country or the world—can reduce even an experienced orator to jelly.

The first time you're interviewed or take part in a discussion on TV will be the toughest. Nothing prepares you for a television studio with its lights and cables and cameras and a seeming multitude of people rushing around doing everything except noticing you. Before you go, get advice from someone with experience about color and pattern of clothes. How you look is important. Man or woman, you'll have to be made-up too, and you'll spend endless minutes just hanging around wondering what's happening.

GO WITH THE FLOW

No matter how nervous you are, no matter how long you have to wait before you're "on," it's essential that you *do not show fear*. It's back to mental discipline again—*you can do it*. Prepare yourself as for a radio broadcast, and from the minute you walk into the studio *go with the flow*. Do as you're told, sit where they tell you, look where they direct, control your nervous twitches, smile, seem interested, and when you have to speak *speak as naturally as you can*.

You'll find that once your first appearance is over, you'll never have the same fear of it again. You might come to find it exhilarating.

THE SECRET

The secret of being as natural as possible in front of a television camera is *not to feel that Big Brother* is watching you, or that there are millions of people critically taking in your every word as well as your appearance. Rather, imagine that you're talking to someone you love. She's sitting at home in front of the television set saying proudly, *"Aren't you doing well!"*

TO RECAP

here are the

easy

ways to help

YOURSELF

STUDY OTHER PEOPLE

Listen to the way they *speak*. Analyze their voices and their delivery. Use your television set.

If someone is boring you, ask *why?*

What is he doing *wrong?*

Is his tonal quality too flat and uninteresting?

Does he keep to the same speed all the time?

Does he fill pauses with "ums" and "ers"; "sort of"; "kind of"; "you know"?

Does she use an upward inflection when there is no question?

Does she sound nervous or lacking in confidence?

Does her face look dull?

If someone is *easy* to listen to, again ask *why?*

What is the speaker doing right? Study the person for pointers on how to hold a listener's attention. Discover how she is able to put information across in an interesting way. You'll become aware that her voice is full of vitality and her face looks alive too, especially her eyes.

STUDY YOURSELF

Acquire an *ear for sound*. When you find yourself slipping into a *monotonous* way of speaking, stop! Take a deep breath and kick off in a more positive way.

Every time you begin a new thought or idea (like a new paragraph) again kick off with a new voice. If you start too low you'll find it difficult to get back on top.

Always remember you can do an enormous amount to help yourself.

However, to help yourself you have to be aware of how you sound, and you do this by actually listening to how you sound.

Before long this skill of studying yourself will become instinctive.

NEVER FORGET THE SIX Ps

The six Ps are your lifeline to good speech. Forget them at your peril.

pitch

pace

pause

power

passion

professionalism

If you're serious about wanting to improve, the six Ps will do more for you in a short time than just about anything else. Get to know them. Become so familiar with them that they pop up all the time and become second nature to you. They'll improve your speech, make you more confident, and definitely move you towards the highest standard.

EXERCISES...EXERCISES...EXERCISES...EXERCISES...

They may sound boring, but what rewards they give you! The old routine of little and often is hard to beat. Do them anywhere at any time. Get into the habit of using unproductive periods of the day to run through them—in the bath, in the car, mowing the grass, lounging in the sun.

PRACTICE PERSUASION

"Sell" all the time—hopes, desires, ambitions, products, the cat... Discover how persuasive you really can be. Keep at it, learn the tricks. Discover the satisfaction you can get from knowing how to put over a good story. Do it sincerely but with flair. Use your new flow of words to describe, cajole, arouse, awaken, encourage, inspire. It's an art that you'll have for the rest of your life.

DISCIPLINE YOURSELF

Mental discipline is the key to getting rid of many errors of speech. The urge to use the "ums" and "ers," and all the others, can be corrected by training yourself to stop before you say them.

Use the pause—it's much more effective. The same applies to that awful upward inflection.

Talking about *the pause...use it!*

It will make an enormous difference in your overall speech pattern.

A pause *before* you say an *important word* creates just the right atmosphere for the word itself to be belted out.

A pause *before* and *after* the word gives it an even greater impact, as though you had put the word in bold type.

But the pause, no matter how tiny, even infinitesimal, will give your speech greater impact.

INCREASE YOUR FLUENCY

We tend to run out of words because at times we can't think of anything to say. Yet *we know them all.* They are in our heads. The distance between our brains and our mouths is very small, but sometimes that distance seems enormous.

So, train yourself. Every time you have a spare moment take a subject, any subject, and talk about it. Don't just think about, talk about it out loud.

A cat, a tree, a road, curtains, politics, religion, sickness, family, feelings, emotions from anger to happiness—each one can become the basis of your own special talk to yourself. In this way, you learn to control your words, make them do what you want when you want.

If you do this regularly, the chances of you running out of words, especially when you're under pressure, is greatly reduced.

THE GREETING AND YOUR NAME

Never forget how important it is to say a greeting and your name with vitality and good enunciation.

The greeting is the first verbal sign we send out. It must have warmth and vitality.

Your name is *you*. People must hear it, grasp it, and be given a chance to remember it. If you mumble your name or say it too quickly or indistinctly they won't catch it. This is particularly true if your name is unusual.

The same principle applies to all words that your listeners may have difficulty hearing.

INCREASE YOUR WORD POWER

Avoid using the *same words*, usually adjectives and adverbs, all the time. Words such as *wonderful, beautiful,* and *nice* are subjective words and don't give listeners a true feeling for what you actually mean.

Use a *thesaurus* to give you a variety of words with a greater definition of meaning. This will enrich your speech greatly.

WRITTEN LANGUAGE

Unfortunately many people still use *written* style language in speech, yet the two are different. While the written word is grammatical, structured, and more formal, the spoken word is easy, flowing, sometimes ungrammatical, less structured, often colloquial, but fluent and, hopefully, eloquent.

Study the two and appreciate the *difference*.

If you have to write a speech it is imperative that you *read it aloud* over and over again until you get the flow of the spoken word.

BODY LANGUAGE

Good body language comes with *confidence*.

People sense nervousness and *lack of confidence* before you even open your mouth. Irritating habits such as ring twisting, fidgeting, or wringing of hands are a giveaway.

If you're *standing*, balance yourself with your feet a little apart. If sitting, make yourself comfortable and don't keep moving—that's distracting.

If you feel like making a *gesture*, do so. If you use a lot of gestures, great. The only time not to is if you're on television when, with the small screen, it becomes annoying.

PROTECT YOURSELF

Everything you do to improve your *power of speech* is a form of *protection*.

We *speak*

to *communicate*

to give *information*

to *verbalize* our thoughts and desires, emotions, and ideas.

We're selling ourselves all the time to our families, our friends, our associates, at home, and in business.

Everybody responds to a good communicator, so it is in your best interest to make sure that you are as good a communicator as possible.

It is worth the time and effort you put into it and it is never too late to begin.

CONFIDENCE

Being a *good communicator* gives you *confidence*.

And you can do it!

This is not **the end,** but rather it's a **new beginning** for you as a **speaker** with

POWER

&

PROFESSIONALISM

THE BRIGHT BEGINNING

The ability to cast off old habits, slothful routines, and dated practices is one to be envied. The bright beginning! It sounds dramatic, doesn't it? Yet it's within everyone's grasp. It's certainly within yours.

With a *little* time spent on yourself, a little *effort* put into how to create the new you, and a lot of *perseverance* to make sure that everything comes together, you can never be a bad communicator. Drag yourself far beyond that cutoff point into the realm of *good, better, best*.

Once you hit on the right formula for yourself, and this varies from person to person, you'll find that your confidence will flow. It will take you to places you never dreamed of and to standards you never thought possible.

CHANGED LIVES

Over and over again during the years I've heard people say, "I never thought I could do it..." But they did, and the satisfaction it brought them changed their lives.

It doesn't matter whether you're a top executive, an office worker, or you stay at home and care for children, the strength you gain from being a quality communicator is invaluable. It enables you to stand up for yourself, to challenge, to exert an influence, to be *heard*, to be appreciated.

But most of all, it releases within you the confidence to do what you want in life, when and how you want to do it. When you've practiced and done your homework, it's *impossible for you to fail*.

READY...GET SET...

It's my ambition that you leave this book knowing that you have absorbed enough information to set you on the right path. It's up to you to put it all in motion, to continue on far beyond what I've been able to give you.

Do it with determination, with an ever-increasing ability and judgment.

Do it with humor and with grace.

But most important, do it with style!